# Queer Voices from the Periphery:

*A Collection of Perspectives from Northeast India*



Editors

**Kaustav Padmapati & Prateeti Barman**

Qurate

quratebooks.com

**Queer Voices from the Periphery:**
A Collection of Perspectives from Northeast India
Kaustav Padmapati & Prateeti Barman

Published by Qurate Books Pvt. Ltd.



Published in 2024



**Cover painting by Arnob Bormudoi**

**ISBN:** 978-81-19263-85-1

qurate
quratebooks.com

**Qurate Books Pvt. Ltd.**
Goa 403523, India
www.quratebooks.com
Tel: 1800-210-6527, Email: info@quratebooks.com

# Foreword

*"We are all human, regardless of our sexual orientation or gender identity. Our emotions, our struggles, and our triumphs are universal. It is only by understanding and embracing our differences that we can truly come together as a community and as a society."*

-George Takei

Queer studies, sexual diversity studies and LGBTQIA + studies have made great contribution in humanising discourses on sexual orientation and gender identity of individuals and group who identify themselves as lesbian, gay, bisexual, transgender, intersex, asexual, questioning and queer in acclimatising us with their life worlds and existential challenges. Historically, they were considered 'queer' (i.e. 'odd') as they challenged the heteronormativity, now 'Queer' is reclaimed as a self-identifier—for non-heterosexual or non-cisgender people. There are intersectional vulnerabilities of caste/ class/ race/ disability/ religion/ region/ ethnicity and gender among the queer community due to multiple marginalities. Many times, their voices are not heard and experiences are not legitimised. Not only that they have to face discrimination and dehumanisation, social stigma and social exclusion in all walks of life.

In this context, the edited volume titled, ***Queer Voices from the Periphery: A Collection of Perspective from Northeast India*** by Dr. Prateeti Barman and Dr. Kaustav Padmapati gains great significance. They have captured the nuances of martial reality of queer persons from Arunachal Pradesh, Assam, Manipur, Meghalaya, Mizoram, Nagaland, Tripura and Sikkim that have representation of rich and diverse cultural legacy of approximately 225 tribes.

## Complexity and multifacetedness of sexuality discourses

Sexuality has been the most challenging issue in the identity politics that include an extensive array of psychological, emotional, physiological and biomedical imperatives contributing to sexual identity, attitude and behavioural pattern. At its most rudimentary level, sexuality refers to a person's sexual attraction to others, and their desire to engage in sexual activity. This can include a wide range of behaviours, from intimate physical relationship to sexual fantasies and desires. At the same time, sexuality is much more than simply a bodily act. It is a deeply personal and intimate aspect of human experience that is shaped by a wide range of factors, including biological (a person's hormones, genetics, physical anatomy), psychological (a person's thoughts, feelings, emotions, experiences and memories) and cultural (social norms and expectations, religious and moral beliefs, and the mass media and popular culture) influences.

Sexuality in the mainstream literature and social theories is mostly portrayed as a source of joy, fulfilment, and self-expression in heteronormative parlance. But, it can be a source of confusion, shame, and conflict who do not fit into the rigid sexual stereotypes. Even now, most of the nation's continue to ban non-heterosexual sexualities and in some countries, practicing homosexuality can lead to capital punishment. Hence, it becomes an utmost responsibility of the human rights movement to decriminalise queer community by amplifying their voices based on their survival struggles for dignity and bodily integrity and make state and civil society sensitive to and responsible for their civil-political-cultural-economic rights and entitlements to be integrated in the mainstream. This edited volume does exactly the same.

## Crucial contribution of this Edited Volume

Introduction by Dr. Prateeti Barman and Dr. Kaustav Padmapati provide the overall framework, highlights and critical reflections on the existing body of literature in queer studies and efforts to create a better space for LGBTQIA+ communities and provide glimpses of their self-mobilisations to assert the rights in the geographical locations of the northeastern states.

**Unit 1** of the volume is dedicated to 'Cultural Discourse and Emerging Dynamics on queer sexuality in Northeast India'. The chapter titled, "Queerness of singlehood in folk cultures of Northeast India" coauthored by Ms. Silba Marak, Ms. Neitsopeu Thopi, Dr. Anjuman Ara Begum and Dr. Samhita Barooah bring out a very delicate concern in our society i.e. 'singlehood' which has gender differential impact.

**Unit 2** of this anthology titled, 'Queer Identity & LGBTQIA+ Movements in Northeast India' vividly portrays the rich history of queer movement. Here, Panna Paul and Somava Das in their chapter titled, "Uncovering the Unsaid "identity," A study of Queer Movement in the North- Eastern Part of India" make the reader understand travails and tribulations of self-organisations by the gender-diverse communities. Dr. Nilakshi Goswami scans social media to make a robust analysis of empowering and demoralizing impact on the queer community in her chapter titled, Queering the Everyday: Northeast India and its Digital Queer Space.

**Unit 3** on 'Homophobia and Cultural Sensibility in Northeast' deconstructs prejudices against sexual minorities rooted in the cultural norms and practices. Dr. Namami Sharma's chapter titled, "Looking beyond the binaries: Examining homophobia in Assamese community"; the chapter by Dr. Prateeti Barman and Alimuddin Ahmed on "Lived Experiences of Gay Men in the City of Guwahati" and Dr Kaustav Padmapati's chapter, "Non-binary Identity & Transgenders in India: Political status of Hijras in Socio-Cultural Spaces of Assam" provide an eagle's eye view of multi faced hardships faced by the non-binary persons in a day-to-day life due to social stigma and lack of family support. Dr. Deepshikha Carpenter's chapter titled, "Gender Obscurity and Homophobia in Northeast India" through in-depth narratives of queer persons succinctly brings to the fore a multi pronged crisis in their lives and their vulnerability in their day-to-day routine activities.

**Unit 4:** 'Queer literature of Assam' makes gender sensitive literary reflections on the texts and their political economy as well as cultural contexts. The chapter titled, "Queer subjects in Selected Assamese

Texts" by Mr. Anupam Hazarika and Dr Stuti Goswami's chapter, "Queer Narratives in Twentieth Century Assamese Literature" acclimatize the readers with Assamese queer literature that focuses on wider spectrum of queer lived experiences and delves on the subversive nature of their queer narratives. Overall, these chapters make us understand the universality of contestations faced by civilization when it comes to gender diversity and gender inclusivity.

## Universality of Challenges faced by the Queer Communities

In a global study done in 2014 of 27 nations, 3% of respondents identified themselves to be gay, lesbian or homosexual and 1% of those polled identified as pansexual or omnisexual.[1] India stood 2nd among them as 9% of respondents identified themselves as bisexual.[2] As per State of LGBTQ+ people in the world, 2022,[3] 67 nations have laws that make private, consenting same-sex relationships illegal. The majority of these nations have laws against "unnatural offenses", "sodomy," and "buggery" that explicitly criminalize male-to-male intercourse. Laws against 'lesbianism, "sexual relations with a member of the same sex,' and 'gross indecency' to criminalize private, consenting sexual behaviour between women are existing in

---

1 Pansexual persons are attracted to other people regardless of their biological sex, gender, or gender identity; whereas omnisexual people who attracted to people of all gender identities and sexual orientations. Sourced from: https://lgbt.ucsf.edu/glossary-terms. Accessed on 2-4-2023

2 Global study on LGBTQ acceptance, available at https://www.reuters.com/business/sustainable-business/global-study-shows-half-lgbtq-people-experienced-threat-violence-last-year-2021-05-17/. Accessed on 1-4-2023

3 ILGA World: Lucas Ramon Mendos, Kellyn Botha, Rafael Carrano Lelis, Enrique López de la Peña, Ilia Savelev and Daron Tan, State-Sponsored Homophobia 2020: Global Legislation Overview Update (Geneva: ILGA, December 2020). https://ilga.org/downloads/ILGA_World_State_Sponsored_Homophobia_report_global_legislation_overview_update_December_2020.pdf Accessed on 4-4-2022.

41 nation states. Lesbians and bisexual women have been persecuted, imprisoned or victimised with arrest even in countries that do not specifically criminalise women. Iran, Northern Nigeria, Saudi Arabia, Somalia, and Yemen are the six countries that have institutionalised the death sentence for consenting same-sex relationships. While Afghanistan, Brunei, Mauritania, Pakistan, the United Arab Emirates (UAE), and the Sultanate of Oman have the death penalty as a legal option for queer persons. The gender identity and/or expression of transgender persons are illegal in 14 countries due to legislation against "cross- dressing," "impersonation," and "disguise." Many more nations have laws that specifically target transgender persons and make same-sex behaviour, vagrancy, hooliganism, and public order offenses crimes.[4]

Thus, we can realise how devastating and destabilising are the effects of homophobia on the gender minorities! Homophobia can cause depression, anxiety, and suicidal ideation among LGBTQIA+ individuals. The stress of hiding their identity, fear of rejection, or experiencing discrimination and abuse can lead to negative mental health consequences. Queer individuals experiencing homophobia are at higher risk of physical health problems, such as higher rates of smoking, substance abuse, and sexual risk-taking behaviours. They face discrimination and exclusion in education and employment settings, leading to lower academic achievement, fewer employment opportunities, and lower earnings. Homophobia can lead to poverty and homelessness among queer individuals, as they may be rejected by their families and face discrimination in employment. Homophobia can cause social isolation and lack of support among LGBT individuals, leading to feelings of loneliness, rejection, and low self-esteem queer individuals face legal inequalities, such as not having the same rights and protections as heterosexual individuals, including marriage, adoption, and legal

4 Human Dignity Trust (2023) Map of Countries that Criminalise LGBT People,https://www.humandignitytrust.org/lgbt-the-law/map-of-criminalisation/?type_filter=crim_gender_exp. Accessed on 17-4-2023

5 Human Rights Campaign (2022) Fatal Violence Against the Transgender and Gender Non-Conforming Community. https://www.hrc.org/resources/fatal-violence-against-the-transgender-and-gender-non-conforming-community-in-2022. Accessed on 10-4-2023

recognition of their gender identity. Homophobia can perpetuate stereotypes and prejudice, leading to further discrimination and brutal violence against LGBT individuals.[5] It can also hinder social progress and prevent the full participation of the LGBT community in society's development.

It is important to note that the effects of homophobia can vary depending on the individual and the socio-cultural and economic context in which they live. Affirmative actions for citizenship rights, legal reforms, representation and voice in the all decision making bodies of politics and governance, and queer-responsive budgeting are the need of the hour.[6] Best practices in Tamilnadu, Kerala, Chhattisgarh in India and in several countries of Asia, Europe, Scandinavia, Latin America, USA, Australia, New Zealand must be shared widely in the communication media. Along with state and non-state institutional responses, we need to change the hearts and minds of individuals through a human-interest approach. Homophobia is a learned behaviour and it can be unlearned by changing the mindset. At the same time combating discrimination, marginalization and violence against LGBTQIA+ people through active intervention and solidarity with sexual minorities for their empowerment becomes a mandate for all citizens.

## Indian Scenario

Homosexuality has remained a taboo subject in the post-colonial India as the British rulers had criminalised consensual same-sex sexual activity under Section 377 of the Indian Penal Code, which classified such activity as an "unnatural offense" and punishable by imprisonment (Indian Penal Code, 1860, s. 377). Now, due to collective efforts of the queer movement this draconian code is repealed. Still, the social stigma leading to social isolation, exclusion persists. As a result, queer persons suffer from mental health

6 Athena Nguyen (2016) Promoting and Protecting the Rights of Lesbians, Bisexual Women, Transgender and Intersex Persons, Canada: UN Women. https://asiapacific.unwomen.org/en/digital-library/publications/2016/05/promoting-and-protecting-the-rights-of-lgbti. Accessed on 12-4-2023

challenges including anxiety, depression, internalised homophobia and suicide. Societal level discrimination in different forms such as job discrimination, housing discrimination, and even exclusion from social gatherings needs to be addressed by public debates and social action. In several states, legal persecution still occurs as there are no laws that provide protection against discrimination on the basis of sexual orientation or gender identity. Lack of support from family, friends, and community organizations can make it challenging for individuals to cope with the challenges of living in a society where homosexuality is considered taboo. We have a long way to go to create an inclusive and accepting world.

I congratulate the editors and contributors of chapters of this book for kickstarting a critical discourse on queer identity and movements from the northeast region of India. This book not only enriches our insights through it evidence based research outcomes but also sensitizes us through in-depth case studies capturing processes and nuances of gender obscurity, relationships and commitment, social interaction, negotiation and communication, homophobia and violence, performativity, closet and exploitation, social role lessness forced by the homophobic gender stereotypes. The book also gives us energy to strive for gender diversity not as a tokenism but efforts towards substantive equality enshrined in the Constitution of India.

I am confident that our collective efforts of rainbow solidarity will bring a new dawn of gender inclusive world as these verses by Lara Jesani convey:

## COLOURS

I glanced at the various shades of blue, in the temporary morning sky,

And all the types of red and orange, when the burning sun went by.

And when the ball of fire set in the sea, I peered at the green waters turn violet,

While the shining star lost itself in the night, I saw the blues and indigos at the deepest.

As the light left without a hint of its presence, I felt the aura emitted by the silver moon.

And in the dizziness caused by the blacks, I sensed the glittering of twilight soon.

As I felt the darkness would swallow me up, And the night would pull the world down,

I saw the magical transformation of colours, from scary black to brooding brown.

Just as this change took away my breath, the dying night was replaced by dawn,

And the enticing colours of nature thus fell, As they went forever on and on.

**Prof. Vibhuti Patel**

Distinguished Visiting Faculty, Impact and Policy Research Institute (IMPRI) and Vice President, Indian Association for Women's studies.

# Content

# Introduction

Gender and Sexuality have always been important and contested areas in definitions of cultural and national identity in the context of a nation state. However, as a typical post- colonial society, the concept of "queer sexuality" and "non-binary identity" is still a forbidden concept of identity in India and in most of the South Asian societies. With the world aggressively marching towards attaining gender neutrality, grasping the difference between 'gender' and 'sex', acknowledging the existence of the third gender or transgender or LGBTQIA+ while simultaneously struggling to validate it, criminalizing discrimination based on gender is barely a surprise in India. Although there are a number of attempts to include queer sexuality and transgender identity in the academic discourse in India, the perspective from northeast on queer or transgender persons voices and identity is a rarity.

The queer space in India is still a contested area, especially in northeast India queer identities appear to be either non-existent or marginalized, acceptance is still awaited. However, a glimpse of the Indian mythology will allow us to understand that role playing, or sex-change is a common, regular and acceptable notion at one point of time in India. According to historian and mythologist Devdutt Pattanaik, the majority of Hindus are familiar with, and quite often enjoy sexually ambiguous stories. However, many of them are still not comfortable with "queer" identities. Although many Hindu philosophers accept the existence of feminine attitude in men and masculine principle in women, Hindu society rejects the idea of public display of alternative "Self." When we talk about northeast India, there are even more surprises. In Manipur, historically within the Meitei community, there are references in the Chronicles of the Meitei kings about an institution of care for the non-binary gender identities. Within the Tangkhul community in Ukhrul District of Manipur, the term 'Yarman' is used to refer to non-binary persons. However, in Mizoram there are no folk tales about someone who is neither man nor woman. Due to the influence of orthodox

Christianity, same sex relations are prohibited in Mizoram. Even for many tribal communities in the region whether Hindu or Christian, same sex marriage is a taboo.

During the colonial period, British rulers ignored the public opinion in the enactment of the infamous Section 377 of Indian Penal Code (IPC) which criminalized gay sex. Section 377 of IPC continued and in 2018, the Supreme Court of India unanimously struck down part of Section 377. It was welcomed by the Indian queer community and many others. However, much more needs to be achieved and at present there is no unified queer movement in India except the Pride Walk organized across some cities. The intersectionality of class, caste, gender and community are the reasons why the queer movement is facing a hurdle like the women's movement in India.

In this background, the queer community of northeast India is looking for their own space. Being considered as India's 'periphery,' northeast part has a total of eight states – Arunachal Pradesh, Assam, Manipur, Meghalaya, Mizoram, Nagaland, Tripura and Sikkim constituting 8 per cent of the country's geographical area accommodating approximately 225 tribes. The culture and customs of these tribes have an important role in understanding the biodiversity and vividness of the region. It is also a region which has experienced insurgency due to various developmental demands and ethnic identity assertion of the people. In this background, when it comes to queer movements, most of the activism remains confined to urban areas. The queer community remained invisible in this region until 2010 due to absence of strong queer activism in the region. Amidst all of this, Guwahati city (Metro Area) in Assam hosted Pride Walks in 2014 and it was the first LGBTQIA+ walk in the entire northeast India. The movement, which started with a handful of people from the community and the support of its allies has grown significantly with the participation of not only people from Assam but also from the other seven states of the region. In 2022, the 9$^{th}$ Queer Pride Guwahati saw the largest gathering of Assam's LGBTQIA+ community and allies.

The edited volume *"Queer Voices from the Periphery: A Collection of Perspectives from northeast India"* is a humble attempt to bring the voices from academia and members of the queer community from the northeast region to focus on the challenges and struggles faced by the members of the community. There are few organizations, collectives and groups working with the queer community in Assam trying to build a network through which charity activities, discussions, counselling are provided. There are a number of queer collectives in Assam which are promoting and advocating extensively queer rights and working extensively to create a space to boost their rights. However, there is a long way to move forward in terms of having a better space and upholding the rights of this community. This edited volume aims to trace the journey of the queer community from northeast India in their various walks of life focusing articles from Assam, Meghalaya and Nagaland.

The present volume comprises essays by a number of contributors from diverse backgrounds from the northeast region. We wish this volume will fill up the gap for the scarcity of literature and research on the queer community of the region. The volume is divided into four units.

The first article *"Queerness of Singlehood in Folk Cultures of northeast India"* under the theme Cultural Discourse and Emerging Dynamics on Queer Sexuality in Northeast India, reflects upon the essence of how queer connotations emerge from choice based or circumstantial singlehood across gender identities. Written by four authors - Ms. Silba Marak, Ms. Neitsopeu Thopi, Dr. Anjuman Ara Begum and Dr. Samhita Barooah from four states of northeast India – Arunachal Pradesh, Nagaland, Meghalaya and Assam- contribute towards a multicultural understanding of how cultural context gets translated to queer identities and their singlehood as a non-binary perspective. The article also explores the popular prejudices, assumptions and ambiguities attached to singlehood from a personal, professional to community and political lens across gender diverse identities. Referring to field research and interviews, the authors try to rediscover the nuanced essence of folk cultures attached to singlehood across genders through the queer theory perspective. The authors sum up that singlehood has become a marginalised identity, pushed to the periphery, as we witness tolerant societies being divided in binaries- heterosexual and homosexuals. Within the heterosexual, the usual man-woman relationship is given a sacred bond and foundation upon this relationship builds a community connected in the form of society or social groups.

The theme of the second unit of the book is Queer Identity & LGBTQIA+ Movements in Northeast India features two articles tracing the identity assertion to having a digital archival space to portray one's identity. The first essay by Panna Paul and Soumya Paul *"Uncovering the Unsaid "Identity": A Study of Queer Movement in the Northeast Part of India,"* discusses the identity assertion of the queer community in the socio-cultural space, struggling against the heteronormative narratives operating against them leading to their subjugation. It conducts a comparative study of the queer movements and presences in some of the states of northeast India, namely Manipur, Meghalaya, Assam and Mizoram, to formulate an understanding of the issues concerning the existence of queer identity in the area. The essay is an interesting take on identity formation in the northeast region with special reference to the queer movement. The identity formation is a complex process and the whole process of creating a "one" identity turns out to be a power struggle between those who have exposure and resources and those who are yet to find a space for themselves, and as a result there happens an indiscriminate erasure of identities which essentially need to be taken into consideration for formulating a holistic queer identity. According to the authors, the queer movement in northeast India is still at a nascent stage and several aspects to look into in the northeast part of India have always been an arena of this politics of identity. The authors present interesting and provocative facts about acceptance of queer culture in four states, for example- gays and lesbians in Manipur though are not ostracized from the society but are always seen as different and face discrimination. The oxymoronic identity is very much evident in the gay community of the state through the existence of the cruising areas of the cities in Manipur.

The acceptance of transgender community in Manipur has come from their traditional roles as *maibis* or *maibas* that is the priests who are transvestites. The silencing of queer identity in the state of Meghalaya and Mizoram, whereas, can be seen as a result of the religious indoctrination under colonial influence. In case of queer mobilisation in Assam is also hampered by this historical power play of dominance and suppression and restrain the support to flow from Brahmaputra Valley to Barak Valley. The two valleys of Assam, Barak and Brahmaputra, have always been in conflict with each other over assertion of ethnolinguistic identity, starting from Assam Annexation in 1826 to Language Movement of 1961. However, we must observe that even though the development of queer movement is different and specific to each state, which make their assertion of queer identity, heterogeneous in nature, there is one strong factor which makes them one and unified under the umbrella of northeast queer movement because all of them developed as an offshoot of the Pan Indian Queer Movement. The queer movement in the northeastern part of India is a testimony of the rise of marginalized from being a state of dejected subjectivity oppressed by multiple layers to a state of exalted subjectivity with a voice unique as well as strong.

In order to investigate the ways in which digital media might offer a counter-space for minority discourses and experiences to be expressed, this essay *"(Un)Comfortably Queer: Northeast India and its Digital Queer Space"* written by Dr. Nilakshi Goswami examines 'The Chinky Homo Project' as a case study. The article uses the in-depth interview with Pavel Sagolsem co-founder of the digital archive to understand its importance. The study offers a contextualized description of LGBTQIA+ lives in northeastern India, where the current social environment is harmful to queer people's mental health, using interviews and digital archival research. The study makes the case that digital media makes it possible to regularly disseminate information on LGBTQIA+ experiences, which can enlighten and shape readers' perceptions of the world. This digital anthology allowed queer people to navigate their gender transitions more easily, and find emotional support for coming out. The digital queer writing is dynamic in quality which simulates reality and helps the readers to comprehend queer experiences sensitively and brings the queer community closer. The article beautifully captures the essence of the project which provides a platform for autobiographical anecdotes and personal trials and tribulations of the queer, but also gives space to self-portraiture at a time when words might not be adequate enough to express one's isolation, despondency, and despair as a "chinky" and "homo."

Although there are so many references to alternative sexuality and queer characters in history, Indian society rejects the idea of public display of alternative "Self." So, homophobia or negative attitude towards homosexuality is widely prevalent in Indian society especially in small towns and rural areas. In the section, Homophobia and Cultural Sensibility in northeast, Dr Namami Sharma in her article "*Looking beyond the Binaries: Examining Homophobia in Assamese Community*," examines homophobia across different age groups in the small towns of Assam. The author observes that the small towns of Assam still harboured the orthodox outlook and homophobic sentiments on the fact of a structured heteronormative society. Age-old notions of equating homosexuality with mental illness or dismissing it as a passing trend are still very prevalent. The recognition of homosexuals with due dignity is yet to be achieved. The younger generation who are exposed to social media and other media platforms are aware of the community and the queer movement. Since the movement is providing a free liberated space for sexual expression, the young adults find it attractive. However, the author is doubtful that this attraction would also lead to the acceptance of alternative sexualities in the mainstream. She suggests that it is high time that the movement touches the small towns and rural areas. It must address the intersectionalities within the society.

Second article "*Gender Obscurity and Homophobia in Northeast India*" in this section by Dr. Deepshikha Carpenter tries to explore the lives of two gay men in a conservative and closeted Assamese society. The two case studies serve as the narrative to explore the challenges faced by gay men living a secretive life. Homophobia and heterosexism are two main reasons being highlighted by the researcher which is hindering the study of gay men in a closed society. The article explores the experiences of violence and exploitations experienced by the participants of the study. Intersectionality of class and gender can be seen in the narratives which is again very pertinent while understanding the queer community's experiences in a closed society of Assam. The article proposes that using constructive social work can help those who are left out by their own narrative by providing them with new opportunities. The role of civil society through various electronic and social movements are emphasized for collective freedom of the queer community.

Another thought-provoking paper in this section co -authored by Dr Prateeti Barman and Alimuddin Ahmed *"Lived Experiences of Gay Men in the City of Guwahati,"* tries to understand the lived experiences of the gay men in Guwahati city and how far they have been able to live their lives to the fullest. Guwahati city, gateway to northeast India, has witnessed the presence of the queer community in public through the pride walk once in every year since 2014. The presence of the queer community in the city of Guwahati is bonded by well-wishers, few organizations working besides the government funded organizations. However, the study reveals that although the gay men solicit partners in various hotspots of the city, most of them prefer to keep their identity hidden. In that process they are subjected to various forms of violence and abuse. Emotional isolation and social ostracism are something common which makes them even more vulnerable. The study also reveals that there is a lack of support system for the gay men in Guwahati. According to the authors, there is a sense of isolation and learned acceptance of violence among the participants of the study. These needs to be addressed by the people working for the queer community so that there is a feeling of inclusiveness, the article suggests.

The fourth article *"Non-binary Identity & Transgenders in India: Socio-Political status of Hijras in Socio-Cultural Spaces of Assam"* written by Dr. Kaustav Padmapati talks about inclusion of third gender in Assamese society. This article critically looks into all aspects i.e., from political to social lives of the transgender community in Assam which seeks inclusion. At present the transgender community is marginalized and discriminated against, which leads to a life without dignity. The author critically traces the presence of third gender even in folk theater of Assam and different Assamese phrases still the recognition of this group of people are nil. Mainstream Assamese society needs to accept and understand the culture, gender, and sexuality of the transgender community, inclusive of their aspirations, hopes, and dreams. According to the author, one of the key challenges is the lack of understanding and acceptance of non-binary gender identities by mainstream Assamese society. Though many positive changes have taken place in various levels there is a need to raise awareness and sensitization programmes about gender diversity and to encourage a more inclusive public sphere where all voices are heard.

In the last section "Queer literature of Assam," two excellent articles on queer literature from Assam, explores the untouched area of Assamese fiction revolving around LGBTQIA+. Queer literature is a new arena in Assamese literature and both the articles tried to look at it critically. Narratives that allow LGBTQIA+ issues and themes and focus on the two important subjects of gender and sexuality create queer literature. Literature in any given society plays an important role and allows us to understand it in a more sensitive way. The first article *"Queer Subjects in Selected Assamese Texts" written* by Anupom Kr. Hazarika looks into three selected Assamese women writers works who have dwelled into the area of queer issues. The article explores that the queer literature in Assam is not a widely researched area, and that most of the existing texts are written by women authors. According to him the presence of queer characters in Assamese literature is a relatively recent phenomenon and Assamese queer literature has not been able to draw scholarly attention. The writer praises the work of Moushumi Kandali's work where the protagonist challenges the gender binary and embraces his queer selves. He also feels that Akashitora's work the protagonists to an extent were to succeed in subverting the gender binary and embrace their queer selves but also get out of experiencing forced heterosexual behaviour. Whereas he is critical about the novel of Manikuntala Bhattacharya's 'Mukti' dealing with male homosexuality for the first time in Assamese literature. In the words of the writer in this novel homosexuality is represented as an aberration, and the reader cannot help but see a misrepresentation of male homosexual behaviour. The moral of 'Mukti' is that either the repression of homosexual desires converts men into pedophiles or all homosexual unmarried men are sexual predators. This article provides an insight into the state of Assamese queer literature and its potential to challenge normative understandings of human sexuality. The writer feels that the authors have attempted to represent queer lives in their writing, and while their attempts are commendable, they are still limited by the norms of Assamese society.

Dr. Stuti Goswami, in her essay *"Queer Narratives in Post-Independent Assamese Fiction"* seeks to find out queer existence in the post-independence Assamese literature. According to the author in the post-independent era, Assamese fiction has undergone several stages of evolution. Within this time frame of post-independent Assamese fiction (that spans roughly nine decades) one witnesses a certain degree of monotony in the depiction of sexuality. Usually, the characters and depictions are of heterosexuality with not much emphasis on rainbow communities. However, there are certain exceptions over the decades and this essay will focus on a few authors in whose short stories and novels there is an exploration of the dynamics of queer existence and relationships. The essay is a synchronic as well as diachronic reading of queer narratives in Assamese fiction in the post-independent era. While attempting to explore the queer narratives, the author also pays special attention to the major social-historical-cultural changes that came over Assamese society after India's independence.

We hope this collection of research articles and essays will pave the way for the readers to look into the queer community of northeast India from a close proximity and create a space of inclusiveness in academia and society as a whole. We are thankful to all the writers for their contributions, without whom this volume would have been impossible. We are hopeful that in the near future we will be able to bring out the next collection of research articles covering all the states of northeast India. A special thanks goes to Prof. Vibhuti Patel for her support whenever we reached out to her. We are grateful to Qurate Books for accepting our proposal on this relevant theme and agreeing to publish it.

**Prateeti Barman & Kaustav Padmapati**

Unit 1

# Cultural Discourse and Emerging Dynamics on Queer Sexuality in Northeast India

# Queerness of Singlehood in Folk Cultures of Northeast India

**Silba Marak, Neitsopeu Thopi, Anjuman Ara Begum and Samhita Barooah.**

## Abstract:

This article will reflect upon the essence of how queer connotations emerge from choice based or circumstantial singlehood across gender identities. It will look into folk traditions of music, stories, performances, weaves, jewellery and attires of diverse northeastern states of Arunachal Pradesh, Mizoram, Sikkim, Assam, Meghalaya, Nagaland, Manipur and Tripura. The study involves feminist methodology of lived experiences and casual conversations through remote ethnography and as per feasibility even offline discussions. Locational advantage of all the 4 authors in Meghalaya, Nagaland, Arunachal Pradesh and Assam will ensure the diversity of understanding of the terms related to queerness and singlehood from a feminist standpoint theory context.

This work will contribute towards a multicultural understanding of how cultural context gets translated to queer identities and their singlehood as a non-binary perspective. It will explore the popular prejudices, assumptions and ambiguities attached to singlehood from a personal, professional to community and political lens across gender diverse identities. This chapter will try to rediscover the nuanced essence of folk cultures attached to singlehood across genders through the queer theory perspective. The connotations of how queerness gets layered and subdued within the cultural norms of customary, religious and ideological practices will also be addressed through this chapter. The saturation of the chapter objectives will determine the actual sample of work. Both primary and secondary sources are explored from a gender inclusive understanding of this work.

**Key Words:** *Queerness, Singlehood, Folk Cultures, Gender Diversity, Northeast India.*

## Introduction:

The essence of writing this chapter together was a journey of revelation. The idea of queerness was the biggest barrier for most of our respondents and the contexts which each one of us represented. Some of us identified with the northeast specificities due to our ethnic, linguistic and geographical identities. The moment we explored the positionalities of the queerness attached to the context of singlehood we were left to oblivion. Our hesitance to address the issues, our own closeted and partially explored selves of singlehood in the queer context made it even more fascinating to ascertain how to proceed through this journey of rediscoveries and resilience. Our ambitious abstract to cover all the northeast states had to be limited to only five states with the hope that there might be a sequel in future times. Queerness is an undefined space which bears no boundaries. It emerged as a slang and restored a deviant identity within the rainbow spectrum of gender, sexuality and gender expressions. One of the fascinating elements of "Queer theory" is its refusal to have a definition. It means to transcend gender and sexual terminologies. Queer theory only agrees upon challenging heterosexuality and heteronormativity. The purpose of this article is to read singlehood as queer in its various transgressions from heteronormativity.

Adrienne Rich (1980) in "Compulsory Heterosexuality and Lesbian Existence" stated that 'women in every culture and throughout history have undertaken the task of independent, non-heterosexual, woman-connected existence, to the extent made possible by their context, often in the belief that they were the "only ones" ever to have done so'(Rich, 1980). Rich also says that these non-heterosexual independent women who did not conform to heterosexual norms were met with in acceptance ranging from "aspersion and mockery to deliberate genocide, including the burning and torturing of millions of widows and spinsters during the witch persecutions of the fifteenth, sixteenth, and seventeenth centuries in Europe, and the practice of suttee on widows in India" (Rich, 1980). Rich also opines that the title of Nancy Sahli's book *For Her Own Good* "might have referred first and foremost to the economic imperative to heterosexuality and marriage and to the sanctions imposed against single women and widows-both of whom have been and still are viewed as deviant" (Rich, 1980). Hence, deviance does not necessarily mean only being gay or lesbian, but also those individuals who refuse heterosexual imperatives or are involuntary victims of heteronormativity.

## Exploring 'Queerness' in Singlehood across different state" specific responses:

While understanding the context of relating to the idea of queerness and its association with singlehood the researchers tried to engage with the understanding from a respondent driven approach. The experience sharing of respondents about understanding queerness from a non-binary and gender fluid perspective was the key to relating to this context. Singlehood was more an identifying category of understanding the nuances where queerness is either presumed or imposed on a single identity of persons of any gender. The understanding of queerness in folk traditions is non-existent in written form but they are evident in conversational references and the terms referred in existing local dialect connotations.

## Nagaland:

Personal interview (Chizami) -1

Who was born female but she acts like men, her hair cut, dresses in men's clothes etc. She stated when she was in class 8 or 9, for her it was natural and never influenced by any external factor, she is attracted to men's clothes and never had a desire for girl/women's dresses. Challenges she faced are from family not accepting and putting a lot of pressure in the beginning but now somehow changed and doesn't say much as she has been like for several years. She said she is also feeling guilty and thinking to change her manly behaviour but it is taking time. Society is not really open or accepting so she is also not comfortable and avoids community meetings/ gathering and church services most of the time.

## Manipur:

Historically within the Meitei community, there are references in the chronicles of the Meitei kings about an institution of care for the non-binary gender identities. Despite the reluctance in acceptance of non-binary relationships, traditionally "Taloisanoba" and "Marupsanoba" relationships of same sex are recognised by the Meitei society. Such cultural diversity remains a silver lining in the struggles of the queer community in the entire Northeast region.[1]

Within the Tangkhul community in Ukhrul District of Manipur, the term 'Yarman' is used to refer to non-binary persons. In a case as narrated by Mr. Z, the clan members decided to keep the property rights for an eldest born male trans woman who decided to be a woman. He shared, "In our customary practice the ancestral land and property goes to the eldest son of the family and now if that son decides to be a woman, then he/she will not get the property but our clan elders decided to give the land and property to her so that such people are respected."[2]

## Mizoram:

'I have never heard the folk tales about who is neither man or woman. These people are treated as special persons which means that if they didn't trap themselves in to attracting their own sexes they were treated as a normal person like one of my grandpa was born within so till now he wasn't married. As a Mizo society our Christianity is the main point that stops us from having sexual relations with both sexes. They treated literally a special person instead of women, men would like to be the one who stops them from acting that way or behaving this way

In Mizo society slang words for hijra' is Tuai' (who are just born within). Who attracts their own sex is 'Mawngkawhur.'

---

1 Santhalambi Leisham Phd Scholar from Manipur in conversation with Samhita through whatsapp and phone.

2 Mr.Zinkhai in Ukhrul district of Manipur in conversation with Samhita during her visit in April, 2022.

How is singlehood understood in the folk traditions of Mizoram? As we are one of the luckiest people even apart from the northeast region singlehood was normalised, it depends mostly on the women's side for the love of their families. They weren't willing to get married for a men due to their health issues (generally a man who got a smaller penis and couldn't get climax during the sex, although his appearance were fine he was neither gay) Regarding cross dressing: We don't have cross dressing, however, they generally wear guys' outfits but they either applied make up or colour on their hair but we could easily make it out. These women are called 'Patil' (women who behave like men.) Out of 5 boys at some point there is one boy who turned out to be an effeminate or homosexual who was called 'an nula ve.' In the context of understanding the queerness in folk traditions of Mizo society, some of the reflections are shared above. The specific terms used are shared by the respondent based on her interaction, experience and prevalent norms of her society. The gender-fluid expressions and queerness attached to singlehood is also expressed in the way a woman's family chooses a man for her.

*Source: Pc Zonunthari*[3]

## Arunachal Pradesh:

Name: MG

38 years from Adi (Minyong) community, Yagrong village, Pasighat, Arunachal Pradesh.

We are five siblings. My mother died a few years ago. My father is alive. I am the youngest in the family. I am working as a teacher and have studied double MA, B.Ed, D. Lit and now studying LLB.

I am single. I don't face verbal abuse directly for being single. However, there is a lot of pressure for marriage. We follow the Dony Polo religion. Our community is ruled by customary laws and Adi Baane Kebang is the Apex body which administers justice.

---

3 PC Zonunthari in conversation with Samhita through Whatsapp.

People call single women as 'Bechari', ' Koi Kam ka Nehi', 'Sahara nehi hai', ' Who will look after you' etc. Single women are also called 'Tumbo' after the death of their husband. Everyday people ask me to stop studying and to get married. I feel irritated. Marriage pressure is very high.

I enjoy my life as a single, and I can mingle with many people. I earn for myself. In our culture women are not given immovable property. Only movable property can be given to girls. I am okay with this system. Because if a girl gets married, her husband will have property. In earlier days, there was a system called 'Appe' where boys and girls from two families were exchanged for marriage. It is not that prevalent now. Domestic violence is very common in our society. Married women face a lot of abuse. Alcoholism, polygamy are big issues that a married woman has to tackle.

## Assam:

In Assam, many connotations are attached to singlehood from a sympathetic or disgusting context. Mostly singlehood is celebrated only when it suffices the family needs, remains circumstantial and community driven. In other contexts, people get curious about the singlehood of either a male at birth or female at birth with labels of many layers. Families are concerned about the future needs of the single people during old age, disability, disease, unemployment and retirement. Markets and consumerism are bothered about the commercial interests in the binary deals of life from properties to livelihood needs. Communities in ethnic groups are conscious about the social, cultural, spiritual, emotional and community identities of people irrespective of their singlehood. Queerness around singlehood is ridiculed in various contexts. Many folk cultures and tales in Assam consider single persons as deviant, peripheral and burdens. The stigma and labelling of queerness of singlehood is so deep-rooted that reimagining lives of individuals beyond their binary constructs remains a longstanding struggle for survival and sustenance.

*Borola, Domora, Eksoliya, Sirokumar and Sirokumari, Keyu Kisu Nuhuwa* (person with nobody and nothing) are the common terms assigned to persons who have transcended the marital binaries. Those who are queer enough to remain single are also framed into terms like *Maikimua* for born male and *Motadang* for born female.

In the Bodo community, persons with single identities are also accepted and included within the society but there are terms attached to non-binary identities. At times *Bolonda* is used for male outcasts and *Lamri* is used for women who deviate from gender binaries. Despite family and binary norms, Bodo community also endorses lifelong neighbourhood friendships outside the marital bonds which are given social recognition. These are friendships for thick and thin times of life. *Bishigi* for men and *Bilwgw* for women to remain part of the extended families and kinships not necessarily from the same clan. It is also a norm to marry a dead single person to a banana tree before his or her cremation. Bodo people also believe that same sex marriages are taboos. The single men in Bodo society are hardly part of any social function and programme. They hardly participate in weddings and other auspicious occasions. When single people die then before cremating, they are married to a banana tree according to the folk traditions of the Bodo society.

In the Sonowal Kachari community also singlehood in people is tabooed in a way that people are hardly included in social and cultural functions.

Within the Mishing community, *Nangladung* is used to depict a single person who sat through their life. If someone is single in the community then they are not given enough societal importance and they are not in leadership roles. They may take up child rearing roles for their extended families and are considered as an eye sore or journey disruptor (jatranasti) most of the time. The transwoman identities are considered as "orudhon" or "tebeli bai" and effeminate men are considered as nang and trans masculine women are known as Mibong Ami.[4]

Within the Hmar community[5] in Dima Hasao, *lengtrûl* is used for the celibate people.

The word *"lengtrûl"* does not have a formal derivation. It became a part of the community language by using it for generations. If traced back to how the word came in vocabulary, it can be cited well with the help of an example. Eg: If we take the example of a paddy field, we can observe that certain sections of the crops are infertile. No man wants infertile crops and are often overlooked. The term *lengtrûl* denotes the same. People who have overgrown or the metaphor of "crops over hosted by weeds", can depict the same.

*Source: Lalramhnem Buongpui, Haflong*

Effeminate:*Tuai*

The word *"tuai"* is slang used for the effeminate person. It can also be traced back as an informal community language. People belonging to this category are seen as unique and unpleasant.

**Tomboy**: *Mi Pa*

The word *"mi pa"* clearly denotes a masculine figure. In Hmar, the men are called *"pasal".* " *Mi*" stands for "people" and the word "*pa*" here is taken from a part of the word "*pasal*", signifying a female who acts like a male. The terminology here also comes in formation as an informal community language.

*Source: As shared by Phoebi, Haflong, MSW student from Department of Social Work in Tezpur University*

4 Jamini Payeng in Majuli in conversation with Samhita through phone.

5 Field Work done by Ms. Phoeibi from Department of Social Work in Tezpur University during her concurrent fieldwork in Dima Hasao district of Assam in conversation through email, phone with Samhita.

## Case Study on Queer Muslim Women from Darrang District in Assam:

While understanding the lives of queerness within the lives of Muslim women in rural Assam, we came across a case study of a lesbian couple whose singlehood became their reason for liberation from the societal structures and family restrictions.

Testimonies of A and J: "No contact with the siblings as they inform home and so I stopped contacting them. The time I got to understand things, I felt that women are treated badly. I remember my father bought a dress and I didn't like it. I cried and didn't like to wear it. Then they bought me a bag of shirts. I was about 4-5 years old. I used to wear my brother's shirts and old pants. However, they didn't say anything.

In school everybody used to call me a boy. I used to like and play boy's games like football and cricket. I used to go to school with boys, not girls. I used to remain silent when girls used to talk about cosmetics and how to look good.

I liked what the boys used to do. I felt bad but didn't say anything. I used to say, 'I didn't become like this. God has made me like this'.

I was admitted to *Muktab* (a traditional elementary school for Muslim) to learn Arabic. I took the Quran and started reading Urdu books. I read half of it. I leant namaz too. I stood first in the Arabic examination at the age of 16. I will pray *naamaaz* once things are settled in life.

In class 9, I observed the boys who like girls. So, I started liking girls too. I liked a girl called 'Manapa'. But she liked me as a friend. But when I see her, I feel differently. I helped her with a project and then she kissed me. I liked it. I didn't kiss in return because it was the first time. But I became crazy for her. We were in the same class. Next day we met again. She was in the science stream, and I was in the arts stream. Once I was writing her lesson in her class and was helping her in her classroom. Teacher scolded me why I entered this classroom when I am from the arts stream. She remained silent and didn't defend me. Since then I have left her. I didn't talk to her for a long time. Only friendship remained but no more love.

I used to be with other female friends, and she used to get angry. So, I wondered why she gets angry with me? I realized we are similar. I told her that I have different feelings for her and she also agreed and then asked if we can be together forever. She agreed. We talked till 3 am that night. We exchanged messages. So, no one in the house got to know of it.

Our conversation and chatting continued except during bathing or eating for nearly three years. We visited each other's house. Family already knew each other. My brother *jonab* used to teach Arabic to them.

In college we keep chatting. I couldn't attend class without her company. Nobody suspected us because they didn't know our class timing. We chatted about family, everything we came to know. We would share our family experience and the restrictions. We were not allowed to wear what we like, what we eat, or what we do.

J: I bought musical instruments worth 20 thousand from savings from pocket money and a loan from a friend. But my brother didn't allow me to learn music. They said it is a sin for a girl. I couldn't open the instruments as my brother would break. My family asked us to leave the house and said that we are bringing bad names to the family.

But still, they didn't know about our relationship. They knew us as friends and didn't like it.

I bought the instruments before lockdown, and I was hiding them in a friend's house. During lockdown, I was feeling bored. So, I brought those back from my friend's house, which made my father angry. We used to meet but there were restrictions. We were facing restrictions on everything we wanted to do. Then I decided to tell my parents about my sexual orientation. First, I told my mother. She understood. But my father did not. He said that it's childish behaviour. They took me to *kabiraz* (local healer) after two days.

The healer tried various methods. He did something in the mud. My parents said that someone has done something to me. They wanted to take me to the doctor but it didn't happen. I faced too many restrictions for being a woman (lesbian).

A: I got in touch with Josh Talks. They got back to me after three months.

We decided to run away from home. We contacted a tailor friend, Amina, whom we used to meet during lockdown and asked for work. She said that she works but is not well paid. Amina said she wants to go to Bangalore and work in a factory. However, for the job an Aadhar card is required. I registered for Aadhar and got an ATM card. Meanwhile, my torture started at home. I can't meet J. I feel depressed as I couldn't meet her. I felt like I was dead. I was not allowed to visit her for 3-4 days. Then, one day she came to shop and she asked me to visit her house. My brother saw it. Once I returned, I showed him waiting with a machete. I asked my sister to pack my clothes and leave. However, my sister in law stopped me. Then I stayed in the house of the elder brother but with a condition that I will leave whenever I want to. My sister in law agreed.

I was working as a tailor and that stopped because I moved to my brother's house because the machine was in my parent's house. Since then I never went. I passed 45 days like this. Then we fixed a date and booked flight tickets on 11 November 2019, at 6-30 am. I lied that I got a job in Kolkata, and I am leaving. I got up at 3 am and had tea. My brother got angry. I said to him you can't stop now as I got a job.

I felt bad when I was leaving my house. Amina's nephew in Bangalore helped us board an Indigo flight at 12.10 pm. It was my first flight in my life. It was a direct flight. We boarded the flight and had a good sleep. I was afraid during the turbulence. There was tension too. J didn't inform home. So, we were tense. After travelling two hours and 40 minutes we reached Bangalore.

Amina's nephew received us and took us to their house.

J: informed her home that she is fine and reached Bangalore. It created chaos.

Her family filed a case against Amina's brother-in-law, Javed. He is a driver. He is a guy. So, he was suspected as well as Amina. He also said that if he is paid ten thousand rupees, he will give information about our whereabouts. So, the family filed a case against him. He was arrested and was put in jail.

After two days, the police called our families for interrogation. On November 17, the police called and so we came back. Javed paid for the tickets since he was in jail. We went directly to Kharupetia police station. Police took us to the Mongoldoi shelter home. We spent one night at the shelter home. Next day they took our statement at 4 PM. We were taken to the Mongoldoi police station and told that we have to go to jail. Our statement was not taken and so we were put in detention. After three days, me, Amina, and Javed got bail.

Her family was planning to make a false certificate as mental patient from Tezpur mental hospital. If I ask for a loan I get abused.

Last few months, I learned a lot in life. Nobody supports us when you are in a bad condition.

J: I was in school. I was 3 years old. I saw different games for boys and girls. I didn't like girls' games. I was attracted to the games played by the boys. I never liked girls' dresses too. It was always under compulsion; I wore those clothes. I was confused why it was happening to me. I hate the idea that I have to be with a man after marriage. I was never attracted to men.

In higher secondary, I came to know more about sexuality. I wanted to know if I am the only one or there are other people like me. Then I thought when my parents arrange marriage, I will let them know. I thought I would die if I got married to a man. After higher secondary, if mom talks about marriage, I used to get angry. Then in first semester I met A. Through chatting I came to know she is probably like me. I can't even tolerate the smell of a boy.

If I want to do something, parents always restrict me.

I turned against ma (mother) that 'ma, you know me well. I am not like other girls. I am like a boy and I never accepted proposals from boys. If you are interested in a man I may not be the same. I feel my body is that of a girl but my mind is like a man. Please don't force me to marry a boy.' I also said that since there is a law on this, it means that there are people like me in this world.

My father said this is absurd. Allah has created only men and women. My brother too didn't like my behaviour and called me hijra, labeling it as a mental illness. My parents started taking me to kobiraj. I didn't like it and it made me crazy.

My father asked for a medical test to show that I am a real lesbian. Where will I get such a certificate? My parents intensified their search for a groom and said that I will get cured after marriage. I started regretting telling it to the family."

*Source: Dr. Anjuman Ara Begum*

## Meghalaya:

"I am 41 and single. People ask me why I didn't marry like you did. I guess I was tempted at one point in my late 20's and 30's to get married, seeing friends and relatives setting up households and stepping into a new life (as they would say). But the prospect of having to share my space and specifically, never being smitten by some kind of true love, as people would say, never arrived for me. I don't regret my decision. I don't identify myself as queer in any categorical way. I've never experienced same-sex attraction. Neither have I been also in love with someone of the other sex, occasional teen crushes exempted. I guess I just like being single."

The above reply comes from a woman who is 41 and doesn't want her identity to be revealed. But she has agreed that the least I can do is give her location as a resident of West Garo Hills, Meghalaya. She says that she isn't an outgoing person and spends most of her time minding her own business. The questions I asked-

"How old are you?"

"Why didn't you get married? Did you ever fall in love?"

"Would you categorize yourself as queer or in simple terms, odd,

because you don't fit into heterosexual category?"

## Analysis-

In the article "Is There Something Odd About Being Single?" published in *the New York Times*, in 2017, Helen Betya Rubinstein talks about her marginalised identity as a single. On seeing a couple fighting in one of her hikes, she feels "conspicuous, as odd and unsettling as a mermaid in the desert." She said she felt queer. In a conventional heterosexual society, such individuals are not given proper recognition. Rubinstein even understood the awkwardness people felt when it came to inviting her to a party as every other guest would arrive with a partner. Singlehood has become a marginalised identity, pushed to the periphery, as we witness tolerant societies being divided in binaries- heterosexual and homosexuals. Within the heterosexual, the usual man-woman relationship is given a sacred bond and foundation upon this relationship builds a community connected in the form of society or social groups. On the other hand, non-heterosexual couples and other sexualities also form their own community groups. Both these binary communities are built upon the foundational aspect of sexual attraction that joins two people. Singlehood, whether it be by choice or circumstance, doesn't seem to fit into either of the two categories.

The subject of the case study resides in the West Garo Hills District of Meghalaya and is single. She does not identify herself as a homosexual but has been assumed by many to be so, because of her singlehood. When I asked her if by being single and not living life in heteronormative terms, she would call herself queer. I explained to her that queer does not necessarily mean gay or lesbian or transgender. It implies a non-heteronormative stance. She thought for a moment and replied that she could be queer, if talked in that sense. But she strongly defended that she was not a lesbian. She did have crushes during her teens but somehow didn't end up marrying anyone like her friends.

In the case of this 41-year-old adult, although her singlehood is by choice and she refuses to be clubbed into any sexual category, she doesn't totally refuse the category of queer. Her queerness owes (she accepts this) to the fact that she didn't get married at all. Her refusal of a social construct, that is marriage, is a refusal of hetero normativity. Secondly, her state as a queer arises because she refuses to embrace the reproductive function assigned to women. Heteronormative societies thrive upon the idea that having children ensures the future. This idea is rejected by Lee Edelman in his "No Future: Queer Theory and the Death Drive" in which he opines that heteronormativity endorses reproductive futurism. Queer, on the other hand, lies at the end of the spectrum. Queer can be associated with death drive, a refusal of heteronormative' s reproductive futurism. Jose Esteban Munoz opposes Lee Edelman and proposes that queerness is actually "a rejection of a here and now and an insistence on potentiality or concrete possibility for another world" (Munoz 2009, 1). For him, queerness is focused on futurity and the not-yet-conscious.

## Conclusion:

While discussing the queerness of singlehood in the folk tradition respondents shared some of their lived experiences. Some respondents were confused about the religious acceptance or non-acceptance of queerness. Most respondents were very concerned about their community's concerns of being or not being queer. Queer identity was associated with either homosexual persons or with the transgender person. Singlehood was separated from the context of queerness as mentioned in the cases from Darrang and Dima Hasao districts of Assam. The very essence of this paper was the undefined understanding of queerness, as it reflects the multiple dimensions of singlehood in different folk traditions within the Northeastern States. This preliminary study does not reference a single entity, role model, or folk context through legends, oral histories, and customs associated with the formation of queerness attached to singlehood.

Non-Binary, gender fluidity, agender and asexual identities are also within the umbrella context of queer spectrum which hardly find space within the transformative, homonormative, bi-normative and heteronormative contexts which could be located within the understanding of singlehood as well. This study has thrown open diverse dimensions for future research possibilities to widen the understanding of singlehood from a pitiful lens to that of a potent discourse.

## References:


1. Butler, J. (2006), Gender Trouble, Routledge, New York
2. Edelman, Lee, (2004). No Future: Queer Theories and the Death Drive. Durham: Duke University Press.
3. Khanna, Akshay, (2016), Sexualness, New Text Publications, New Delhi.
4. Munoz, Jose Esteban. (2009). Cruising Utopia: The Then and There of Queer Futurity. New York: New York University Press.
5. Rich, Adrienne, (1980) "Compulsory Heterosexuality and Lesbian Existence". Signs. Vol. 5, No. 4. The University of Chicago Press.
6. Rubinstein, Helen Betya, (2017), Is There Something Odd About Being Single? New York Times, available at : https://www.nytimes.com/2017/10/27/style/modern-love-is-there-something-odd-about-being-single.html

Unit 2

# Queer Identity and LGBTQIA+ Movements in Northeast India

# Uncovering the Unsaid 'Identity': A Study of Queer Movement in the Northeastern Part of India

**Panna Paul and Somava Das**

## Abstract:

Northeastern part of India is an area of conflicts and confrontations. Identity conflicts as diverse as ethnic, racial and linguistic, are always at the forefront in ascertaining the sociological position of the spatial scenario of this part of India. There are ample amounts of discussions and discourses that are mobilized on these areas of identity conflict as well as there has been assertion of these identities. However, in midst of all these discourses, the 'queer identity' has remained silent and submerged, it has remained as the subaltern identity to the mainstream culture and can be seen as facing the double marginalisation. They can be seen as what Sandip Roy calls as "double minorities" where they are first marginalized for their identity as someone belonging to the northeast region and secondly for their queerness. This paper focuses on the identity assertion of the queer community in the socio-cultural space, struggling against the heteronormative narratives operating against them leading to their subjugation. It conducts a comparative study of the queer movements and presences in some of the states of northeast India, namely Manipur, Meghalaya, Assam and Mizoram, to formulate an understanding of the issues concerning the existence of queer identity in the area.

The paper by drawing on the identity conflict theories of social identity, prejudice and stereotyping has tried to locate the presence of the queer identity and the extent of their 'assertion' in the northeastern part of India, on the basis of some primary data collected over a period of two months from various queer activists, queer people, allies and even the queer migrants who have moved out of the state or have moved in from other states. The paper for its study has also considered the media coverage of the issues of the northeast queer community as their primary data. The paper is devised as an attempt to niche out an intersectional subaltern status of queer movement of northeast India.

**Keywords:** *Northeast India, Queer Movement, Double Marginalisation, Identity conflict, Subaltern narrative, Intersectionality.*

## Introduction:

*"I wish I could live a life like those I see in the Pride parades of Kolkata, I want to participate once there to take the feel of how they live freely and kiss each other on streets"* said Bappa (name changed) *(Personal Communications,* 2021) a 26 year old respondent who identifies himself as a gay man from the Karimganj town of Barak Valley of the state of Assam while looking at the photos of Pride Parade of 2019 on Facebook. Why this assertion? Why is this very idea highlighted at the very outset of a paper that is concerned about queer identities from northeast states? The answer to these queries is a simple word "difference", to be more precise "disparity". The disparity of identity formulation of being a queer subjectivity is the very reason that has made this assertion by Bappa significant here in this discussion. In spite of being identified as queer, he cannot relate himself with the queer subjectivities placed at a different geo- political space, in this case the cosmopolitan nature of the metro city of Kolkata. In order to find a solution to this, the very aspect of identity needs a brief deliberation.

Peter Weinreich (2013) defines the concept of identity as a concept which, "construes oneself in present expresses the continuity between how one construes oneself as one who was in the past and how one construes oneself as one aspires to be in the future" His definition asserts that an identity is not an independent entity and does not take shape on its own rather it takes into account the totality of the individual's encounters with past and its aspirations of the future to describe the way it presents itself in the present. Thus, the identity is not innate or indispensable rather is a constituted prospect of one's individual projection. One of the important ways through which this identity is constructed is the relationship of an individual with the society and social structure in which it lives. Henri Tajfel (1979) refers to this constituted identity as the social identity.

Social Identity according to Tajfel (1979) refers to a person's sense of who they are based on their group membership. It is this belongingness to a certain group which becomes an important source of pride and self-esteem for that person. In order to increase the self-image one enhances the status of the group to which it belongs. Thus, there appears a division of the world around them as 'us' and 'they', there happens a categorization of insiders and outsiders by the members of that group. This categorization is often guided by the hypothesis that the in-group members bear all the positive aspects of the world and the out-group for them symbolizes the negativity of the world, as one can see in the colonial polarization of Orientals and Occidentals. This polarization happens because the members of the out-group fail to meet the normative scenario and ideals of the in-group which make them see the out-group as inferior and downtrodden.

The polarization is often guided by the prejudices that the in-group develops in their ideological setup relying on the difference and also leads to the stereotyping of the out-group members. This according to Tejfal (1979) happens on two levels firstly by exaggerating the differences and secondly by highlighting the similarity of group members. There arises a conflict of identity between the in- group and the out-group. This conflict becomes more intense when the in-group member holds the power and asserts its supremacy over the members of the out-group. Herein comes Foucault's (1978) proposition of repressive hypothesis which states that anything that stands in opposition to the discourse in power, which in this case is the social identity of the in-group members, tries to repress it or silence it. Thus, emerges the whole issue of politics of identity, which is concerned with resentment of the members of the out group to assert their identity against all odds created by the members of in group who seems to have power in hand to exercise.

Politics of identity, thus, may be defined as a phenomenon that arises out of shared experiences of injustice and marginalization of certain sections of the society. It occurs when some ethnic groups or social minorities find themselves as oppressed, marginalized and feel that their uniqueness and distinctiveness are under threat from the majority group. In such a situation, there is collective mobilization within the group with a view to secure their distinct identity.

Identity politics tends to portray differences and grievances rather than similarities and bonds among groups and individuals. It refers to a process of self-construction and self-presentation of group traits like race, culture, religion, ethnicity and gender with a view to secure social recognition and legal concessions. Thus, it is also identified as the politics of 'recognition' (Burns 2006, p. 150) and the politics of 'differences' (Young 2001, p.18). The politics of identity thus can be seen as what Foucault (1978) describes as the relational concept of power where when a power is exerted on a group an equal amount of power is reciprocated by them. The conflicts of identity in that way can be seen as the power exertion by the out- group over the in-group in order to assert their identity as unique and valid. In the context of the present paper the identity which is dominant and assertive is the patriarchal idea of heterosexuality which pervades over the social structure as well as formulates various institutions of societal structure and the identity that is in conflict is the queer identity of the non–heterosexual community.

The mapping of queer movement in India through the lens of this politics of identity is a difficult arena of discourse and deliberation because the movement as Shradda Chatterjee (2018) points aims at universalizing the queer subjectivity and there is constant effort towards achieving a homonormativity on Indian standards in order to foster a foundation of homonationalism. In this endeavour the very movement loses its core purpose of putting forth the voices of marginalized as queer in this context appears to be a dynamic aspect which finds articulations upon each utterance. In their attempt to create a unified and homogenous discourse of queer narrative, the expressions of various other aspects like race, colour, creed, caste and ethnicity which go into formation of an identity are overlooked. Each expression of queer is centered on its cultural and historical legacy, it is the result of its interaction with past and expectation of future, and it becomes problematic for them to correspond to an identity which is foreign to them. This assertion with power creates a rift and leads to the suppression of those identities. This whole process of creating a "one" identity turns out to be a power struggle between those who have exposure and resources and those who are yet to find a space for themselves, and as a result there happens a indiscriminate erasure of identities which essentially need to be taken into consideration for formulating a holistic queer identity.

The homogenous queer identity enforces a discourse which lays down the structure for defining who can be queer and who can't be and herein the movement assumes a capitalist supremacy which is initially the institution against which the movement aims at fighting with. It is at this juncture the whole queer movement of northeast India comes into limelight. The movement in northeast India is still at a nascent stage and has several aspects to look into. Northeastern part of India has always been an arena of this politics of identity. The conflicts of identity have always remained an issue of great importance for the region. Ethnic identity has been at the foundation of identity politics in the northeastern part of India. Many of the states like Mizoram, Meghalaya or Nagaland have come to existence because of the identity assertion by the group which has felt marginalized from the mainstream culture of India. Apart from this, the conflict of linguistic identity is also an important area of concern especially in the state of Assam where the state is divided into two linguistic groups Assamese and Bengali, and they are in constant conflict with each other. There have been many efforts to formulate an all-inclusive identity for the northeastern part of India, with a motive to break away with the stereotype of the identity being just a block. Eminent scholars like Sanjay Hazarika, Dhruba Hazarika, Sipra Sen, Sanjib Barua and others, through their works have tried to draw a parallel history of the northeast in order to formulate a record of the identity conflicts in the area. "Prof. Udayan Misra's (2014) book *India's North East: Identity Movements, State, and Civil Society,"* explores the alienation that northeastern people face from the mainland governance and it is this alienation which flared the demand for autonomy based on ethnic, linguistic or tribal identity. However, in the midst of all these the identity politics that remains silent for a huge period of time is the conflict between the queer and the heteronormativity in society.

The queer community in the northeastern part of India is also not free from the inhibitions that it faces at the mainstream, but the mainstream queer culture has never taken into account the issues and matters related to the queers of this region until recent times. In that way the queer community of the northeastern part of India turns to be a subaltern within the queer struggle itself. There happens to be an intersectionality operating in their operation where they are first oppressed as queers and secondly, they are rendered invisible and also silenced in the movement because of their identity of northeasterners. This paper will attempt to locate this identity and its presence as well as assertion within the greater queer movement of India as well as within the diverse identity politics of the region. The paper has taken up four major states of the region for the brevity and the clarity of the paper; they are Manipur, Mizoram, Meghalaya and Assam.

The methodology used for this paper is basically concerned with the analysis of a body of data that have been obtained through some secondary sources including media coverage by various news portals, magazines, articles published in journals, books, about the queer scenario of northeast India and also some primary data which has been collected through personal interviews from the various states and various parts of northeast India. There has been an efficient synthesis of data to develop arguments and also to find a resolution. The methodology has been a blend of both conventional and contemporary techniques to carry on with the logical progression of argument and give a detailed study about the queer scenario of northeast India with reference to above mentioned four states.

Manipur is a one of the states where women acquire a respectable and important position in the society. They can be seen as controlling the economy, politics and even religion, but even then, they are not free from the impositions of the patriarchy. A study by Samant Roy (2017) reveals that among all the states of northeast, maximum numbers of female workers are registered from Manipur in secondary and tertiary sectors respectively. As per the NSS (National Service Scheme) data of 2018-19 labour force participation for women in urban areas is 29.8 %, which is higher than national average of 22.5% and in rural areas it is almost same as national average. They can be seen as the victims of the patriarchal normative structures of the society. The nude protest of the women folk at Kangla in protest of the brutal killing and rape of 34 years of Manoroma Devi or the case of lifelong hunger strike of Irom Sharmila Chanu against the Armed Forces Special Power Act (AFSPA), although present a picture where women enjoy a very powerful stature in the society, at the same time one of women who was paraded naked admits that she has been feeling guilty about it and feels that while standing for her folks she has been disloyal to her duties (Rehman 56). Thus, one can see that in spite of being able to get politically involved, she has not been able to come out of her roles prescribed by the hegemonic ideal of femininity. The naked ladies are first seen as mothers, a traditional role prescribed to them by society and then their use of body as a means of protest is highlighted. Thus, one can see that patriarchy has been one of the important decisive factors for determining the status of social structure in Manipur. It is this hegemonic ideology which is also responsible for the oppression of queer in Manipur.

Gays and lesbians in Manipur though are not ostracized from the society but are always seen as different and face discriminations. According to Kumam Davidson (2016), a queer activist from Manipur, homosexuals in the state live a dual life like most of the cities. The oxymoronic identity is very much evident in the gay community of the state through the existence of the cruising areas of the state. The Kangla gate is one of the well-known cruising areas of Imphal city, the capital of the state and the cruising takes place in the late hours of the night, when all heterosexual activities come to seize. Kumam (2016) mentions that the guys who visit these places make efforts to hide their identity. They do not divulge even their names to the person with whom they hook up. However, regarding lesbians, Kishalay Bhattachajee (2013) refers that lesbianism is accepted to a certain degree in the society, because of the all women bond being very prominent in the social structure of the society. Though it is not talked about much in the society, however, they are often dealt with a lot of tolerance and acceptance. Manjusri Chaki Sarkar (1984) is of the opinion that female friendship is casually accepted among the people of Manipur. She arrived at this observation after she saw many women sharing intimate relationships among them even to the extent of excluding their men in some cases. Pavel Sagolsem, (2016) a gay rights activist from Manipur and a youth consultant with Breakthrough says, "There are fairly a lot of gay and bisexual men who seek relationships and look for good company. The support system runs deep, and the networking isn't on a basis of right-based struggle but on a sense of community that runs strong as a group of friends, peers, brothers, etc." According to them the invisibility of gays and lesbians in Manipur is tackled by technology.

In recent years, another organization called Ya-All! is working towards creating awareness and creating a support group for the gay men and lesbian women at grass-root level. Sadam Hanjabam, the founder of Ya-All in a private interview with us revealed that, "the invisibility of the gay men and lesbians is solely because of the importance earlier organizations gave to transwomen and M.S.M.S concerning HIV, as funds could be easily arranged to work." While talking about the sense of alienation among the queer youths of Manipur in the Pan India narrative he pointed out that "my identity as an open gay man has provided them with a model to look for, they could see me and understand that they also have a community to rely back on" *(Personal Communications,* 2021). There has always been a narrative of exoticism and insurgency about the tribal youth at the pan Indian level and it has already pushed them to the fringes of mainstream India, tagging them as subalterns. Under such circumstances, it becomes even more difficult for a queer subjectivity from such a geo-political space to find a space of safety and it finds itself as double marginalized and acquires the status of sexual subaltern. According to Sadam, it is this gap that needs to be filled up to create a queer discourse for Manipur or northeast in broader sense. The process has however started as he points out how they are concerned about creating support through sports and has come up with the world's first Transgender football team. *(Personal Communications,* 2021) The state of Manipur is also the state which has shown a lot of acceptance towards the transgender persons or the transvestite persons.

The acceptance of transgender community in Manipur has come from their traditional roles as "*maibis*" or "*maibas*" that is the priests who are transvestites. They are given huge respect in the society and often revered as most holy souls in the society. Thus, the mythological and cultural association of transgender or transvestite people has rendered their acceptance in the society. The study of queer scenario in Manipur brings the reference of the predominant transgender identity of the state known as "*nupi manbis*" or "*nupi saabis*", as pointed out by Dr. T. Deepa Manjuri (2004). The word literally means "women like". They are treated as honourable equal citizens of the state, pursuing their vocations and are also achieving great success. In year 2008 a community-based organization called All Manipur Nupi Manbi association was established. Unlike in other parts of India, many within the transgender community in the state work in the beauty industry and have been able to create economic viability for themselves. Santa Khurai, a transgender activist and a member of the organization said that, "the transgender persons have had a very visible presence in Manipur." However, after the Naz Foundation judgment of the Supreme Court in the year 2014 a new organization called "Empowering Trans Abilities" has been formed in the state and it aims at providing a safe space for queer women and trans men to socialize among themselves. Immediately after the Delhi High Court's verdict in NAAZ vs. Government of Delhi NCT in 2009, a non-heteronormative marriage took place in Manipur. The group noted that the marriage is more social in nature, and no legal marriage certificate has been issued after the marriage. These organizations also organize an annual transqueen festival which on one hand shows the liberal space of the state of Manipur towards them and at the same time reveals the weakness of the movement which is promoting the normative idea of beauty and commoditization of beauty. According to recent reports a transman from Manipur named Bishesh Huirem has won the title of International Transqueen contest for the year 2016 in Thailand. According to Subhojit Dutta, a queer activist from Assam and a member of Xukia the level of acceptance in Manipur is comparatively more than any other northeastern States *(Personal Communications,* 2021). It is evident in the ways the administration is working towards their benefits. In Manipur, the collaboration between Manipur State Legal Services Authority and the CBOs resulted in many workshops regarding the legal challenges faced by the transgender persons. A Transgender Welfare Board has been formed in Manipur. The state also registered a few successful stories after the formation of the transgender welfare board.

However, the living conditions of queer community have undergone a great change in the recent few years in the state of Assam. The issues of queer subjectivities of state gained national attention when Xukia came into existence, and they started to organize awareness campaigns. The period before Xukia, has been a period of anonymity and ignorance for the queer community of Assam. In the year 2012, there has been a report in the Assamese daily about the suicide of two girls together by drowning in Brahamaputra. In spite of the incident being a result of homophobic trauma, which has been later on recorded by Xukia, the newspaper as well as the parents, remained silent about the matter. The formation of Xukia in the state has given a strong and powerful voice to the LGBTQAI+ community of Assam. The first ever protest in the favour of the rights of homosexuals was organized independently by some women on 16$^{th}$ December,2013 as Global Day of Rage against the Supreme Court order to recriminalize consensus same-sex activity. But talking about the protest to *The Times of India,* Miguel Queah states that, "*There were homosexuals in Sunday's event but they are afraid to openly proclaim their sexual orientation.*" It reveals the invisibility and the fear that works within the mindset of the homosexuals in the state. It is Xukia which has provided a safe and vocal platform in Assam for them to come out. One of the important works of the organization in the state is to organize the Annual Queer Pride Walk in Guwahati, Assam.

In the February month of the year 2014 Xukia organized its first ever Guwahati Pride Walk. However, they received a lot of backlash for this. The office of one of the supporting NGOs is vandalised by some right-wing radical members. Some of the participants received threat calls. On the day of the pride, a few members of Hindu Yuva Chatra Parishad, a right-wing student party, tried to stop the pride but were arrested by the police. The local newspapers while reporting the event said that in the land where Goddess Sati's vagina has been worshiped, the queer people will never allow masculinity to survive and flourish. Another newspaper even has gone to the extent that the sexual drives of the queer people have brought them on roads to find new victims. These reports reveal that the intellectual elite of Assamese society has been predominantly homophobic in nature and mainly because it has hurt the patriarchal heterosexual ideology of society which relies on the phallic power to survive. The presence of Goddess's genitals can be seen as leading to the castration of the male authority in the land which is coming out as a frustration to those whom they see as different to heterosexual norms. However, in spite of all these, according to Abhisekh Chakraborty, former member of Xukia, the pride walk has been greatly successful in creating a unified platform for the queer community in Assam and over the years it has grown tremendously. Thus, in the year 2015 the organization has been successful in organizing Northeast Pride Walk bringing participants from almost all the seven states of northeast. Bitopi Dutta , one of the founding members of the group while talking to the First Post regarding pride walk reveals that, "*The response was very good. Xukia enabled us to create broader conversations around LGBT rights in Guwahati, which was hardly a thing before...*"

One of the only changes that came in Assam after the 2009 verdict of Delhi High Court is that the queer community has gained great visibility in various cities of Assam. One of the group members notes that after the 2009 verdict, the four groups which used to organise social gatherings of queer individuals before that path-breaking verdict made them bolder. However, visibility doesn't always ensure safety – so the more visible the community becomes the greater is the harassment and backlash from different conservative groups. Deshabandu Club of the state is working for the upliftment and rights of Men Having Sex with Men, which is MSM. It thus takes into consideration a group or a matter which is very much specific to the Indian queer scenario. The mobilisation of community in Assam was, however, slower as compared to Manipur and Meghalaya. According to the participants from Assam this is due to the strong presence of right-wing organisations across the state.

The situations have taken quite a different shape after the decriminalization of Section 377 on 6th September 2018, as more and more community members have started to come out of closet and ascertain their identity. However, in the absence of a well-defined and established support network they are often left clueless and rendered helpless in dire situations. It is at this juncture Xomonnoy has its inception in Assam, whose sole purpose is to mobilize the community people and provide all sorts of aid, legal or mental, to the members in need. The working of Xomonnoy has added new dimensions as it renders its services to remote areas as well. But in doing so as Shivlal Gautam, one of the founding members of Xomonnoy, points out that they faced many problems, for instance conveyance, funds and even stereotypes surrounding queer community. Shivlal while talking in an intimate private conversation opines that he finds it more difficult to mobilize people in Barak Valley (a place predominated by Bengali Speaking population) than in Bodoland in spite of having the same language of communication. The discussion added another dimension to the queer mobilization in Assam *(Personal Communications,* 2021).

The two valleys of Assam, Barak and Brahmaputra, have always been in conflict with each other over assertion of ethno-linguistic identity, starting from Assam Annexation in 1826 to Language Movement of 1961. There is an atmosphere of distrust and malignity between the people of these valleys which is always fostered and fed up with political gain. This voluntary enemy creation for power play takes over every aspect of one's social, cultural and personal entity and acts as a hindrance in their progress. In case of queer mobilization is also hampered by this historical power play of dominance and suppression and restrain the support to flow from Brahmaputra Valley to Barak Valley. The people from Upper Assam are always seen with a gaze of doubt in spite of the fact that they are all queer subjectivities. This problematises the Queer Identity formulation which is subjected to a harassment common to all the community still finds it difficult to find them with home with queer belonging to different socio-linguistic identity. This makes it evident that queer as a marker of identity is a dynamic aspect. It is this dynamic quality that led to formation of another queer organization called SAGE :Barak Queer Collective to work for the community members of Barak valley. Though there is so much development, Shivlal is of the opinion that the queer movement in Assam is still at nascent stage and there is a regret that they have not been able to produce the next line of leaders to carry forward the movement in Assam *(Personal Communications,* 2021) .

The silencing of queer identity in the state of Meghalaya and Mizoram, whereas, can be seen as a result of the religious indoctrination under colonial influence. The colonization of the British Empire in the northeastern part of India has been more about ideological domination rather than power imposition. The Colonizers have brought with them missionaries who deceive the innocent tribal folks into adapting Christianity. This adaptation has led to the extinction of the pagan culture, of which queerness can be seen as a part and parcel, and adapting a culture which is not their own. In this adaptation they have also adapted the homophobia which has been instilled in him through the religious doctrine of Christianity, which sees homosexuality as a sin (Gandhi, 2002). Leela Gandhi (2002) points out that it is not the homosexuality that is adapted from the west, but it is the homophobia which has entered Indian society from the west. In Mizoram organizations like Mizo Zirlai Pawl (MZP), Young Mizo Association (YMA), Mizo Hmeichhe Insuihkhwam Pawl (MHIP) and Mizo Upa Pawl (MUP), have started programmes in the state to identify homosexuals and to "take action" (Chouhury, 2015) against them because they firstly consider it against the ethics and teaching of Bible which sees it as a sin and secondly it is also based on the assumption that it is against the culture, an intricate argument to defend heterosexuality.

Even the Presbyterian Church of Mizoram, the largest church-denomination in the Christian dominated northeast, has decided to snap ties with the American Church associations when the American Government has provided the queer people with the marriage equality rights. While covering this story for *The Sunday Guardian*, the synod secretary at the Presbyterian synod executive committee (SEC) told the reporter that, "We feel that going against the teachings of the Bible, as against losing fellowship and funding, is more harmful in the ministry of our church". The SEC also issued a decree to excommunicate gay members who were living with same sex partners, as long as they lived with them. A Mizo gay man while speaking to *The Wire* (2015) says that, *"We have a sexual urge for the same sex. But we can suppress this sexual urge if we put our WHOLE FAITH in JESUS CHRIST and of the fact that CHRIST had killed all of these humanly desires when he was on earth (sic)".* He claimed he had been 'born again."

While organizing a seminar on homophobia in Aizawl, Rev Rajkumar observed that the LGBTQAI + community in Mizoram are brainwashed into believing that they are living in sin. "They've been forced to believe that because of their sexual desires", he told *The Wire*. He also said that they have faced more opposition within their own faith from other denominations than from other religions. Many churches from the northeast region wanted to de-link from them in this dialogue. Mr. Cub (a profile on a popular Gay dating App) while talking expressed , *"I know I have many of my acquaintances who are gay , but we are afraid of the Lord to speak that out."* This fear is instilled in them through religious indoctrination as Rev. Rajkumar (The *Wire*, 2015) pointed out. He further expressed that they could hardly get scope to explore themselves and many of his friends have migrated to the nearby town of Silchar, in Assam to "*enjoy in the name of studies*" (Cub, *Personal Communications*, 2021). This adds another dimension, the migration of queer subjects, which is also a common phenomenon in the northeast, to find a safe space and to get a "feel of the life" as pointed out by Bappa. However, it is more seen in the states with more rigid religious and traditional laws like Mizoram and Meghalaya.

Meghalaya also suffers from the same problem in the silencing of queer identity. In Meghalaya, a Christian-dominated state, homosexuality is a word that is better not uttered. However, that does not make the state devoid of homosexuals; a general term used for lesbian, gay, bisexual and transgender, or LGBTQIA+. The prevailing homophobia or fear of homosexuals, and castigation by religious bodies compel many to remain closeted and follow the dictates of society, the "natural" way of life. Rev NS Phawa of Khasi-Jaintia Presbyterian says homosexuality is a strange concept in the Khasi community. Samakami, a community-based organisation (CBO) located in Shillong has been offering health services and legal aid to members of the queer community since its opening in 2007. There is also a concern about the educational and economic empowerment of marginalised LGBT populations in the state. One of the important discourses responsible for the miserable condition is religion. In spite of being a matrilineal society, where women hold the key to economy, patriarchy has been successful in making its visible presence. It is evident in the widespread homophobia in Meghalaya's social structure. Raymond, a member of Shamakami while talking to *The Shillong Times* expressed that if he comes out to his parents, then his parents as religious members of the church will be traumatized. Rebina Subba, who is also a lawyer, says that the resistance from the church is so strong that when she started *Shamakami*, she threatened to shut down the NGO. For religious groups, anything other than heterosexuality is "abnormal" and a "disease".

"Transgenders people here do not like to be referred to as hijra. This is a common mistake that people, including those in the media, make," says Rebina Subba, founder chairperson of Shamakami while talking to *The Shillong Times.* The term which is used for the transgender is *Hic Mulier* which literally means manlike woman. The transphobia is evident in this where they are seen as a copy of something and nothing innate in their existence. Twenty-seven-year-old Dona says while talking to *The Sunday Times,* though her family has been supportive, society hasn't been. Talking about acceptance in Shillong, Dona says, "As long as one follows the conventional ways of dressing and living, there is no problem.

Once you rebel and try to come out of the shell, then all hell breaks down." The story is similar for other members of the community. Nelly Ryntathiang, who was born in Lumlang, says the church refused to accept her way of dressing like a woman when she was a child. She recollects that, "I was called a sinner and a shame to the society. I was asked to leave the church when I was 13. The reaction was same in school,"

However, in the next year after the NALSA Judgement of the court, on July 2, 2010, the MSM and Transgender project was launched in the state of Meghalaya, the first of its kind in the state and in the entire northeast region of India. A group called Seringue was launched in 2010 in Shillong. The organisation works towards the rights of lesbian and bisexual women and transmen. They have held several programs with Sappho for Equality. Many of the tribes in Meghalaya are matrilineal and the property generally goes to the youngest daughter of the family. There are then particular issues related to the gender identity of that youngest daughter and the property rights. This includes questions such as what happens when the youngest child is a transwoman. The member felt that since the customary laws are very strong, strong advocacy work needs to be done in this regard. Thus, they started awareness programmes and campaigns in Meghalaya which have been able to bring about a lot of change regarding the position of the queer community in the state. In spite of all these efforts, only little could be achieved regarding the provision of a safe space for queer subjectivities because even after the read down of Section 377, the members of the community are denied permission to hold a pride rally in Shillong in 2018. While talking to one of the residents during the lockdown period of 2021, he expressed that " it is better to stay in Delhi than to move back to Shillong , because neither I will have any job nor any freedom to live the way I am in that small house of two rooms." (Joe, *Personal Communications,* 2021). This declaration further adds to the scenario that how shallow the space is for the queer people in Megahalya, even after such a long period of mobilization.

The discussion so far about the development of queer movement in northeastern India with reference to states mentioned have brought forth some striking observations which need to be deliberated over for drawing out a culmination of the arguments which have set the tone of this discussion, which is the politics of identity and the subsequent assertion of that identity. One of the interesting breakthroughs about the politics of identity in northeast India is that the politics of identity for northeasterners have a heterogeneous and homogeneous aspect to it. Within the designated geo-political space of 'northeast' the fight is heterogeneous, as every ethnic, language, and tribal group is trying to assert its exclusive supremacy over the diverse democratic setup, and the aspects of identity around which the politics is practiced is also variegated. On the other hand, outside the geo-political space of 'northeast', the fight is between the homogenous identity as a northeasterner and the common Indian identity. Thus, in both the cases the 'ingroup' and 'outgroup' are different because of the different circumstances they operate within and situations they are the result of. The nascent queer movement in the northeast also has these dual aspects to it. The development of movement in various states has different and unique inceptions to them. In other words, the foundational platform for the development of queer movement in different states is different, making this fight for identity heterogeneous. If the state of Manipur is taken into consideration, as mentioned by Sadam Hanjabam, the impetus of the queer movement in Manipur has been derived from the culturally institutionalised aspect of transgender subjectivities, called as *Nupi Manbis or Nupi Sabis (Personal Communication 2021).* The beforehand established discourse around the transgender has helped in creating dialogues about other queer identities and to mark their presence distinctly in the socio-cultural fabric of the state. Even the support building for the community members are different in the state of Manipur. The annually organised Transqueen Contest by All Manipur Nupi Maanbi Association under the leadership of Shanta Khurai is a significantly important step towards bringing together the queer community of Manipur. It was only after four years of this contest that the state saw its first pride parade. According to Sadam, games like football and traditional arts like Shumang Leela,

Raas etc also play a great role in creating support groups (*Personal Communication,2021)*. On the other hand in the case of Assam, the movement saw its inception in the incident of the Supreme Court's ruling out of the Delhi High court's decision of scrapping section 377 in the year 2013.

According to Shivlal, a queer activist from Assam, the first ever queer gathering against the Supreme Court's ruling out of the Delhi High court's decision of scrapping out of section 377 was spontaneous and not a planned one and is mostly by gay men and women (*Personal Communication, 2021).* The movement in Assam was started by gay men unlike transgender persons in Manipur. The cosmopolitan temperament of the urban areas of Guwahati city made the movement develop further by following the global footprints of the movement, as the very idea of Xukia is the brainchild of Bitopi Dutta later on Milin Dutta, an Indian transman with American citizenship, who wanted to develop a model similar to the model of queer support group of the United States of India. The procedures followed for developing the support group are inspired by methods used by Pan Indian groups like Harmless Hugs or the Humsafar Trust. The methods include holding meetings, pre pride preparation meetings, pride walk, discussions, etc. However, in Assam the movement is centrally concentrated to Guwahati, and to some other Urban spaces like Tezpur, Dibrugarh, Jorhat etc within educated elite class. The efforts to reach grassroots level have recently begun under the initiatives of Xomonoy. However, regional disparities among the urban spaces are also evident in Assam, as the movement could not create any impression in the Southern part of the state. In other words, the Assam from the point of view of queer movement is the microcosm of India with its uneven proliferation. It is this cosmopolitan nature which has made organizations like Shamakami to work for the issues of queer under the garb of HIV in the state of Meghalaya, before any of the states of Northeast. The presence of the queer movement and activities surrounding queerness are minimal but are very much evident in the state.

Even though, the development of queer movement is different and specific to each state, which make their assertion of queer identity, heterogeneous in nature, there is one strong factor which makes them one and unified under the umbrella of northeast queer movement because all of them developed as an offshoot of the pan Indian queer movement. As has been said by Sadam Hanjabam, founder of queer support group Ya_All , that the people of northeast could not relate to the activities and identity assertion of pan Indian queer movement, there is no one who could provide them with a role model. This very feeling made them marginalized to greater extent even with the queer community and made it hard for them to accept themselves. It is at this juncture that different states of northeast started to organize them in their own way (*Personal Communication, 2021).* Shivlal is of the opinion that the queer movement in northeast is to nascent to have its own unique features but it ensures to make a well-defined voice for those who are not only neglected and oppressed by 'out group' of heterosexuality but are also marginalized because of their geographical identity within the community itself (*Personal Communication, 2021).* Thus, the politics of identity prevalent among the queer community of northeast, is the politics of recognition as mentioned by Young (2001), as this fight for expanding the scope of social identity, struggle is to find a space which is based on equality devoid of any discrimination. In that sense, this identity politics is strategic and voluntary, with essentialist tendencies so that the queer community could be saved from a triple level of marginalization, first as northeasterners, second as queer and third as queer from northeast. When on one hand certain states are making efforts to progress, there are also certain states which are yet to enter the arena of recognizing queer identity. Mizoram as a state is still in the slumber of medieval catholic ideology making it hard for the queer movement to have its inception. The deep-rooted Christian indoctrination has made it strenuous for the queer movement to develop.

Thus, to draw conclusion it can be said that in spite of all the discrimination that they face mainly because of two dominant discourses at work in the region, patriarchy and religion, they are able to carve out a niche for themselves. The protest against the oppression is very much evident in the formation of various support groups like Xukia or Shamakami and also in the involvement of the state authority in it as evident in Manipur and Meghalaya. The queer community in the northeastern part of India has also been able to make a place for itself within the mainstream queer movement, as evident in Xukia's organization of dialogues, an LGBTQ film festival based in Kolkata, West Bengal, the participation queer activists from the region in the Queer Leadership Summit organized by pan- Indian organizations like Harmless Hugs or The Humsafar Trust. Thus, it can be said that the identity which has always remained unsaid and unheard because of its difference from the dominant discourses of identity at practice is gradually uncovering itself in a greater realm of hopes, aspirations and negations as pointed out by Sudip Dey, "when I left this state 10 years back, it was a suffocating space where I could hardly breathe. But as I see now the avenues are opening up and I could see young and old people to a great extent asserting their identities..." *(Personal Communications,* 2021). Sudip Dey identifies himself as a 30 years old Gay man and he stays at Bengaluru city but belongs to Silchar town of Assam. The gradual growth of queer assertion in the northeastern part of India has been able to bridge up that disparity of the identity formulation of queer subjectivity and has tried to strike a balance of between the mainstream queer narrative and northeast. The queer movement in the northeastern part of India is a testimony of the rise of marginalized from being a state of dejected subjectivity oppressed by multiple layers to a state of exalted subjectivity with a voice unique as well as strong.

## References:


1. Bhattacharjee, Kishalay (2013). *Che in Paona Bazar: Tales of Exile and Belonging from India's North East.* New Delhi: Pan Macmillan.
2. Burns, Lynda. (ed.). (2006) *Feiminist Alliances.* New York: Rodopi. 2006.
3. Chatterjee, Shraddha. (2018) *Queer Politics in India: Towards a Sexual Subaltern Subjects.* New York: Routledge. 2018. pp: 12-34
4. Choudhury, Ratnadip. (2nd October 2015). Mizoram NGOs to 'cleanse' society of homosexuals *The Deccan Herald.* Available at URL: https://

www.deccanherald.com/content/504044/mizoram-ngos-cleanse-society-homosexuals.html

5. Dutta, Abhinava. (2016). *Listening to Multiple Voices: Sexual Minority Activists Speak.* Kolkata: Solidarity Foundation.
6. First Gay Rights Rally in City. (16th December, 2013) *The Times of India: City.* Available at URL : https://timesofindia.indiatimes.com/city/guwahati/first-gay-rights-rally-in-city/articleshow/27465045.cms
7. Foucault, Michele. (1978) *The History of Sexuality: Volume I : An Introduction.*
8. New York: Pantheon Books.
9. Gandhi, Leela. (2002). Love Well: Homosexuality and Utopian Thought in Post-Colonial India. *Translating Desire: The Politics of Gender and Culture in India.* New Delhi: Katha.
10. "Gay & Happy People." (4TH December 2017) *The Shillong Times.* Available at: URL: https://theshillongtimes.com/2017/12/02/gay-happy-people/#:~:text=Sigmund%20Freud%2C%20in%20a%20letter,be%20 classified%20as%2 0an%20illness%E2%80%A6
11. "In Conversation with Xukia: A Queer Collective in Assam.( 22nd May. 2017). *Feminism in India. Com.* URL:https://feminisminindia.com/2017/05/22/xukia-queercollectiveassam/#:~:text=Xukia%20is%20an%20informal%20 youth,which%20was%20organised%20by%20Xukia.
12. Kumam, Davidson (5th April 2016). Exploring LGBT Life in Manipur's Imphal. *Gaylaxy: Empowering Expressions.* URL:https://www.gaylaxymag. com/articles/queer-voices/famous-kangla-gate-middle-city-manipur
13. Manjuri, Deepa T. (8th Februray 2004) Gay Studies in Manipur: Points to Ponder. *E-Pao.*. URL:http://epao.net/epSubPageExtractor.asp?src=news_ section. opinions.Gay_studies_in_Man ipur_-points_to_ponder
14. Rahman, Raiful Alom. (10th June 2017 ). Queer Pride: In Northeast India, the movement for LGBT rights is gaining visibility. *First Post. Available at* URL: https://www.firstpost.com/india/queer-pride-in-northeast-india-the-movement-for-lgbt-rights-is-gaining-visibility-3537421.html
15. Sarkar, Manjusri Chaki. (1984) *Feminism in Traditional Society.* New Delhi: Shakti Books.
16. Sithlou, Makepeace. (9th December 2015). A Theological Challenge to Christian Homophobia. *The Wire.,* Available at: URL:https://thewire.in/rights/a-theological-challenge-to-christian-homophobia
17. Tajfel, H., & J. C. Turner, (1979). An integrative theory of intergroup
18. conflict. *The social psychology of intergroup relations.* Monterey: Brooks/Cole.
19. Weinreich, Peter. & Wendy Saunderson (ed.) (2013). *Analysing Identity: Cross Cultural, Societal and Clinical Contexts.* New York: Routledge.
20. Young, Iris Marion. (2001) "Equality of Whom? :Social Groups and Judgments of Injustice" *The Journal of Political Philosophy. Vol : 9 Issue : 1.* UK: Blackwell Publishers.

# (Un)Comfortably Queer: Identity and Belonging in Northeast India's Digital Space

**Nilakshi Goswami**

## Abstract:

While discussing queer identity and their rights, one usually focuses on the disticntion between the much sidelined or purposely underplayed concepts of gender and sex. However, in considering sexual orientation, gender identity, and expression of the queer population of India, the Northeastern region of the country[1] continues to languish as an unacknowledged site of queer experience. Thus, the goal of this paper is twofold. First, with an emphasis on The Chinky Homo Project (2018) – a digital anthology of queer writing from the Northeast, the aim here is to extend an understanding of digital archiving as increasingly gaining attention and giving space to erstwhile muted queer voices. Secondly, it outlines how far digital space, in its capacity both within and outside, foregrounds a space for queer subjecthood and queer expression while generating a dialogue and creating peer support for heterogenous queer identities among different sub-communities from the Northeast.

**Keywords:** *Queer, Digital Media, Northeast, Identity*

## Methodology

The present paper is based on the doctrinal method of qualitative research. A comprehensive review of existing literature, journals, and reports, mixed with newspaper and magazine articles, is primarily relied upon in order to frame a distinctive understanding of the current position of the queer people in the constitutional law regime and its

---

1 Northeast India would be henceforth referred to as NER (Northeastern Region of India) unless mentioned otherwise.

invisible conflicts with societal perception in rapid pace of modern social and legal developments. Considerable attention has been given to the in-depth interview with Pavel Sagolsem, the co-founder of The Chinky Homo Project, conducted in January 2022, which has provided significant insights into the problematic interpersonal dynamics of acceptance and expression of queer identities of NER in the digital space. This paper begins with an analysis of conditions of possibility that births the emergence of queer representations in the internet culture, followed by an examination of the interplay between regional and local/global processes that drive the contemporary queer politics of queer individuals from the NER in India.

## Queer Identity in India and the Northeast: An Introduction

While the United States, and the West at large, is traditionally credited for introducing the contemporary lexicon and praxis within the LGBTQ+ liberation movement, anthropologists have long recognized Southeast Asia as a region that possesses multiple indigenous forms of gender diversity (Peletz 2009). From the hijra communities referenced in mythology to the androgynous deities like Ardhanarishvara, for centuries India has witnessed gender-nonconforming identities interwoven into its social and cultural fabric. However, it is much later, in 2014, that they were legally recognized as a "third gender."[2] In 2018, after decades of activism, section 377 of the Indian Penal Court (IPC) was ruled out as unconstitutional, resulting in the decriminalization of consensual homosexual acts between adults in India[3]. Despite the growing significance of gender pluralism, which includes intersex people, transgenders, eunuchs, and hijras, among others, and changes and challenges to the law in India, gender nonconforming people have been profoundly affected due to a lack of social recognition. This has brought about strict enforcement of gender binaries in society, consequently, not just subjecting gender nonconfirming subjects as

2 See Nanda, Serena (1999), Neither Man nor Woman: The Hijras of India, Wadsworth Pub. Co.

3 Rao, Rahul (2020). Out of Time: The Queer Politics of Postcoloniality. Oxford University Press.

unintelligible but further equating these rigid expectations with moral virtues. While media coverage of gender non-conforming people has substantially increased over time, their portrayal often continues to be stereotyped, and the media and popular culture tend to fetishize them as deviant, deceptive, and threatening to society. These negative stereotypes, in turn, have transmuted them into elements disrupting the social "order," while implicitly validating violence and social biases against them as normal.

Queerness[4] already has a history of being put under erasure, outlawed, or sanctioned against—the title of the paper playing upon this "(un) comfortably queer" rendition of the identity. The situation seems to be worsened when considered within the context of the Northeastern region of India, which has always found itself in a multiply jeopardized position[5]. The NER—always already excluded from the mainland—has more often existed in the peripheral imagination of the larger Indian society due to manifold reasons: cultural, geographical, and historical, among others. Amidst this, the poetics and politics of queer sexuality further take a backseat. Drawing together both queer and phenomenological perspectives, this paper focuses on the reflection of everyday queer lives of Northeast India through its critical orientation in digital space. Addressing the online queer narrative blog The Chinky Homo Project, founded by Kumam Davidson and Pavel Sagolsem, as a case study, this paper delves into how the digital space has been appropriated to explore, document, and archive the personal struggles

---

4 Queer" is a word with a long history and a complexity of meaning. From its origins as a pejorative, it has been reclaimed in recent decades by academic and popular communities alike. At its most basic, "queer" operates as an umbrella term: a marker of identity differentiated from "gay" or "LGBT" in that it encompasses all non-normative expressions of sexuality or gender (Grace, Hill, Johnson, and Lewis). Not every person whose identity falls within this category identifies as queer, and "queer" itself is a contested term. Within the context of queer studies, the concept of queerness has been interpreted and reinterpreted in manifold ways. At the same time, queerness is not an abstract concept. Even when it is applied conceptually, queerness is still rooted in the embodied realities of queer subjects. In this paper, queer is being used as an umbrella term for sexualities and gender identities beyond heterosexuality and/or in reference to radical political formations in relation to such identities.

5 See Baruah, Sanjib (2020). In the Name of the Nation: India and its Northeast, Stanford University Press.

as queer and Northeastern in India. The argument here primarily rests at the intersection of digital humanities and queer thinking, examining how the queer community has deconstructed the legacy of "normativity" that clings to the metaphor of the everyday realm. Where is the queerness in digital humanities? How does The Chinky Homo Project enables the exploration of new ways of thinking? Why "Chinky" and why "homo"—how are these fundamentally reductive terms inverted as a source of immense empowerment?

While racial microaggressions and stereotyping of the people of NER by the rest of the country has become an everyday reality, a study commissioned by the Indian Council of Social Science Research (ICSSR) (2020) found that "Northeast India seamlessly fits [an] Indian's imagination of a Chinese person." This indicated how physical appearance played a significant role in reinforcing prejudice against them. The study further confirmed how people from the region "faced an increased number of acts of hate and prejudices against them" (Singh, The Hindu). The numerous insurgency-related issues in the region have further strengthened the stereotypes of NER as a conflicting land mired in hostility and violence. Production and reproduction of these stereotypes have robbed the people of this region of their history and identity. In regions of conflict, the focus on violence is so immense that the everyday lives of people inhabiting the region is often disregarded: their every struggle for livelihood, their desires, their negotiations with the politics of the everyday. The state often seems to have more grave issues to deal with, viz., insurgency, unemployment, and substance abuse, to name a few. Amidst this ragtag and bobtail of concerns, the politics of gender and sexuality takes a backseat because of its subtle, nebulous, and unnamed nature.

Queer writings from the Northeast, erstwhile muted, however, now seem to exist at the heart of the digital space. Situating the queer voice in the convergence of culture and digital technology is a significant aspect of the evolving engagement with the paradigm of Digital Humanities, be it in terms of amplifying queer visibility through online communities, being heard in social media platforms, or documenting queer cultural narratives and representation in digital archives.

With that knowledge in mind, the paper elaborates how The Chink Homo Project documents the often-disregarded queer narratology through the workings of digital narratives. Analyzing the virtual space through the phenomenology and political economies of new media as a crucial site for queer activism remains pivotal here. This paper, thereby, critically examines how far digital space foregrounds a place for alternative narratives of the queer selfhood, highlighting the potential of these platforms—the internet and the digital media—for assertion of identity, belonging, and solidarity. By doing so, it further interrogates to what extent does Digital Humanity fosters inclusivity while enabling minority identities like queers in resisting oppression and challenging heteronormative frameworks.

## Queer Lives in Archives: Why Visibility Matters?

The Chinky Homo Project documents a series of memoirs, memories, testimonials, photo stories, among other digital narrative series, centering on different approaches toward queer stories online. The testimonies of several queer persons on this online platform primarily revolve around their personal experiences and the idiosyncrasies of their struggles as a Northeastern in India, usually referred to as "chinky" in a racial slur, and as queer–often catcalled as "homo." Inevitably, a series of commonalities emerge through the conversations and narratives documented in this digital archive, where queer people from the NER are getting out of silos and coming together as communities.

Archives could be perceived as repositories of not just what aspects of culture and history are constructed, preserved, and disseminated, but also what is excluded. Imbued with power, considering how it is involved in the values, biases, and intent of those who control the contents of the archive, they can be perceived as a critical lens extending an understanding of the relationship between history, power, and identity. As Arjun Appadurai argues (2003), an archive is a step towards the creation of an alternative memory and "a tool for refinement of desire" (24-25). It could then be stated that archives have implications for different kinds of social and cultural change, where marginalised groups can create, preserve, and share narratives and create alternative perspectives that do not find a presence in the mainstream. The motif of queer visibility, the centripetal force of this digital anthology, The Chinky Homo Page, then presents itself as both the opposites: as a breakthrough as well as a challenge. In one hand, visibility might lead to exposure; on the other, it could result in providing solidarity and a strong sense of community between people previously unaware of the existence of individuals with shared queer identity. The fact that this microblogging of self-representations, all curated as a part of one single category in The Chinky Homo Project, helps in underlining the similarity characteristic of different approaches to understanding queer identities. This increased space, appropriated as a strategic tool, further makes it likely for the NER Queer Community to find a niche group that reflects a similar struggle, needs, and values.

Since time immemorial, sexuality has been interwoven with space, and queerness has been historically relegated to a liminal physical presence within societies, whereby politics of visibility had played a crucial role. However, what remains at stake under the whole idea of "invisibility" is yet to be interrogated, especially concerning the virtual and digital space of LGBTQ identity. To make sense of the queer internet presence like the one initiated for the Northeastern queer people by The Chinky Homo Project, it is imperative to historize similar digitally interactive platforms established in the past. In the 1970s, the historian John D'Emilio (1983) states how the movement for the rights of the homosexuals was heavily characterized by "silence, invisibility, and isolation" (1). The very first Pride march of its kind in the United States, the Christopher Street Liberation Day March in 1979, organized in New York, could be considered one of the several strands of the commencement of the LGBTQ equality movement. The iconic chant, "Whose streets? Our streets!," which appeared in that Pride march, has been consistently used as a rallying cry by different lesbian and gay organizations of the 1970s. Similarly, the LGBT movement cries of the 1970s United States— "Gay is good!," "Come out!," "Out of the bars, into the streets!," to name a few—centered around the fundamental idea of visibility. Followed by this, rallying cries like "Out of the closet, into the street!" by ACT-UP in 1987, "We're everywhere!" by the Lesbian Avengers in 1992, "We're here, we're queer" by Queer Nation in 1995, evidently prove how LGBT movements since their very inception, framed their strategies of resistance and agendas around visibility and recognition (Darsey 1991). However, merely emphasizing the politics of visibility for all LGBTQ was not enough, especially for disadvantaged sections of society and ethnic groups, including women, people of colour, the disabled, the economically deprived, among others. The claims to public visibility and space often made by activists were made from a privileged white position (Hanhardt 2016). As discussed by the noted feminist philosopher Linda Martín Alcoff (2005), neoliberal, racially driven, and ableist cultural frameworks of American society are chiefly "dominated by the realm of the visible." (6). Alcoff further states how this is "indeed revealing significant facts about our cultural ideology, but that what the visible reveals is not the ultimate truth; rather, it often reveals self-projection, identity anxieties, and the material inscription of social violence" (6).

In a similar vein, the politics of visibility, with reference to the representation of LGBTQ of the NER, is fraught with tension owing to the racial microaggressions and stereotypes of the rest of the mainland. However, queer spaces have become increasingly dominated by and predicated on internet technology and digital platforms. Cyberspace could be seen as a protective and liberatory space released from the stringent heteronormativity, pointing towards the urgent concern of visibility with renewed importance. It is within this context that The Chinky Homo Project could be located: giving visibility to the lived local experiences and narratives of people living on the cusp or at the intersection of both subjectivities—gender nonconformity and the NER, both the state of being and belongingness considered sexual and regional "other." Recording the testimonies, fictions, photo essays, and other such diverse forms of digital expressions of individuals who identify themselves with the queer community remains the pivot of this digital archive. It underscores the glaring distinctions between contemporary forms of expression and the nearly invisible queer voices, be it in terms of the dearth of queer representation in the region's literature or broader discourse within the country. The politics of visibility foregrounded in this digital space transcends the mere act of being observed or being seen. Rather, it refers to a radical refusal of the queer to be a part of a system that denies their recognition, stifles their narratives, and denies their civic recognition. Visibility and spaces of visibility and identity, however, cannot stand alone but require recognition alongside it. Merging the politics of visibility with recognition, Sarah Ahmed (2006), the queer theorist, discusses the "politics of hope" as crucial to queer politics.

> . . . queer politics would have hope . . . but because the lines that accumulate through repeated gestures, the lines that gather on skin, already take surprising forms. We have hope because what is behind us is also what allows other ways of gathering in time and space, of making lines that do not reproduce what we follow, but instead create new textures on the ground. (569-570)

## Being Queer in Digital Spaces: An Exploratory Analysis

What does being queer embody in digital spaces? How about the challenges with regard to self-presentation and disclosures? How far do the affective forms of virtual/digital/online belongingness forge and sustain minority identities? As evident in The Chinky Homo Project, first, digital space has allowed queer people access to information and resources, representation, and self-revelation in ways that were not possible in the pre-internet era. Pavel Sagolsem, one of the co-founders of The Chinky Homo Project, talks about how the internet brought the community closer[6].

> Digital is the new interface for young people—a primary reason we [Davidson and Sagolsem] chose digital. Moreover, it has better outreach and is easily accessible for everyone. But what is it that we are trying to achieve through this project?

6 Goswami, Nilakshi (2021, January 29). Personal Communication with Pavel Sagolsem [Interview on Zoom].

What are the social changes we want to bring through it? First and foremost, we wanted to start talking about the representation of queer people from the Northeastern region, both at home and in the diaspora, and the digital space made way for readily accessible information. For a lot of queer people at home, growing up was such an isolating experience. That's the reason we focused on building an anthology; a digital anthology, trying to build a conversation, trying to build a database of experiences where we could advocate for the need to politicize these experiences.

Secondly, the mobile internet is where young people live and dwell on. And there is a lot of information on queerness online. However, when we came out and started exploring, the kind of material that we could find was from other regions, other cultures. We could feel how the sense of isolation we felt while growing up could go away only when you find stories of your own region. And that is what we do in this digital space. Within this space of The Chinky Homo Project, we provide the platform for an observed conversation[7], as opposed to a fleeting one. When we talk about The Chinky Homo Project, we talk about the origin of it on the basis of individual experiences; also, at the same time, the kind of solidarity-building that happens among Northeastern students when one gets into the political and activist spaces.

For Pavel, it seems the digital anthology allowed people to navigate their gender transitions more easily and find emotional support for coming out, which Pavel terms as "observed conversation8, rather than a fleeting one"[9]. This could be, then, read as a substitute for community support networks, considering the challenges of coming out in person at the onset of one's transition. Additionally, digital spaces like The Chinky Homo Project could be

---

7 Emphasis mine.
8 Emphasis mine.
9 Refer to the excerpt from the interview with Pavel Sagolsem, co-founder of The Chinky Homo Project, 2022. Goswami, Nilakshi (2021, January 29). Personal Communication with Pavel Sagolsem [Interview on Zoom].

further read as crucial spaces not merely in navigating but also in asserting one's identities. Considering how digital space allows easy alternation of names, gender, or appearance without any social constraints, it has the ability of providing refuge from the stifling impositions of the physical world. In other words, due to its inherently flexible nature, online platforms such as The Chinky Homo Project then offer the opportunity for queer communities from the NER to experiment with different facets of their identity, free from discrimination of any sort. It is noteworthy to mention how the distance and anonymity provided by the virtual world not just extend a space from rigid gender binaries but also a sense of safety in the process of one's self-discovery. Discussing the features of cyberspace, Stephen Whittle (1998) argues how "the body or its performativity is no longer the dictator of gender. Gender has become who or what you experience as actual – what you choose to represent as you type at a keyboard, nothing more" (395). Whittle further states how exploring one's identity in cyberspace can foster a sense of authenticity in the real world while potentially driving activism (395). Shapiro, in a parallel context, contends that due to ease in mobilization, digital space has the capacity to manage strategies required for queer activism (2004).

Exploring the manner in which digital humanities overlap with queer studies remains a promising site for contesting the prevailing, and hence accepted, notions of meaning-making. Digital tools, considering their distinctive ability to incorporate more integrative elements, enable narrative techniques that ensure better visibility to queer representation and history, simultaneously ensuring a more engaging experience for the readers. At the same time, it is of paramount importance to examine queer identity in digital humanities so as to encourage a deeper engagement with the inclusive facets of digital humanities. The chapter, thereby, aims to highlight an alternative perspective within the discourse of digital humanities that gives precedence to multiple facets of people's identities and social justice as much as data and other computational while foregrounding the complexities of queer subjecthood and its evolving interpretations.

While the intention here is to foreground a more inclusive vision for queer epistemologies in digital humanities, the purpose is not to direct a specific approach it must embark on. On the contrary, the resolve here is to introduce achievable alternatives and put forth ideas that foster dialogues on queerness within the digital humanities as a realm of imaginative potentiality. While The Chinky Homo Project's move towards queer digital humanity automatically implies affirmation of queer experiences and perspectives within its practice, the research delves into how it further addresses tangible techniques in approaching the manner queerness can alter the practice of digital humanities itself.

Amongst several projects on digital humanities focusing on queer identities, many are found to appropriate the well-recognised DH practices, including preserving historical documents (archiving) and creating vivid visual data (visualisation) in order to ensure mass accessibility of information regarding the social, political, and artistic history of the queer communities across. The digital interactive project Lesbian and Gay Liberation in Canada (LGLC) remains a notable example in this context. This online space has amassed a consolidated database ranging over 34,000 events and contextual essays for its users. It also offers a dynamic map that is interactive in nature, while enabling its users to locate the notable figures shaping the creation of queer history, along with the significant sites and historical events spanning from 1964-1981[10]. There are similar kinds of DH initiatives exploring queer counter histories, like the "Texting Wilde" (TWP) project launched at The Centre for Digital Humanities, a collaborative research innitiative at Ryerson University that digitally archives for its users the biographical narratives chronicling Oscar Wilde's life and work before 1945[11]. The Chinky Homo Project could be read in a similar paradigm of discourse: digitally documenting and archiving the experiences and the politics of the everyday life of queer people of Northeast India, who, more often than not, find themselves in a

---

10 Lesbian and Gay Liberation in Cananda (1981), lglc.ca

11 Texting Wilde: A Biography Exegesis Project (2012), https://www.ryerson.ca/centre-digital-humanities/projects/texting-wilde/

doubly jeopardized position, both as a "homo" and as a "chinky," which this digital anthology curtly destabilizes. A project like The Chinky Homo Project uses digital humanities methodologies to subvert the normative ideas associated with identity and self-representation. Autobiography, as a genre, which is typically based on the idea of representation of a coherent self, in this case is, however, defied in its representation of non-heteronormative and queer identities. While doing so, it reveals the multifarious ways of meaning-making within queer identities, dismantling the often-hegemonic understanding of the subject while exploring issues ranging from social discourse to creative expressions, revealing the social and cultural dynamics of cyberspace.

The project not only provides a platform for autobiographical anecdotes and their personal trials and tribulations but also gives space to self-portraiture at a time when words might not be adequate enough to express one's isolation, despondency, and despair as a "chinky" and "homo."

**Figure 1.** Photo excerpts from "Being Quarantined in a City all by Myself: Photo Story," The Chinky Homo Project, Oct 2021.

In a manner similar to the Surrealist photographer Claude Cahun, who explored gender identity and the subconscious mind (Goswami 2018), the photo story here epitomizes the attitude and style of the subject of this self-portraiture as they stare at the camera somewhat defiantly with an outfit that conventionally looks neither masculine nor feminine. The monochromatic hue of the image on the extreme right of the panel portraying the hand of the subject reaching out to the open indicates the desire to keep one's identity no longer hidden. This particular photo-story calls out the intersections of ethnicity, race, and queer identity specific to the Northeast Indian diaspora. The economic uncertainties looming large during the pandemic hit resulted in the rise of return migration from the cities to the rural hometowns. Following the nationwide lockdown and the sealing of inter-state borders, queer people from NER, however, chose otherwise. Defying the trend of reverse migration, they chose the freedom of the city towards their sexuality over the prejudices and hypervisibility their hometown offered, as evident in Figure 1. hus, in a way, The Chinky Homo Project has demonstrated how the digital humanities have the ability to directly address the intersectional issues of representation and self-representation and, in turn, portray how each corresponds to and, in turn, is influenced by each other. Another narrative in The Chinky Homo Project recounts the everyday experiences of a trans *Potloi*[12] *artist, a profession reserved only for cis women. While her narrative voices her challenges and obstacles as a transgender person committed to this profession, it also* expresses her everyday struggles during the pandemic (Figure 2).

**Figure 2.** Images extracted from "Pandemic Diary of a Trans Potloi Artist," *The Chinky Homo Project*, August 30, 2021.

12 Potloi is the traditional bridal wear of Meitei Hindu women in Manipur.

According to Jack Halberstam (2008), the subcultural queer community in the current times requires a "nuanced theory of archives and archiving" (41) to address the intersectionality of their lived realities. Discussing the growing and nascent queer cultural frameworks theorising archival documentation, Halberstam further iterates the significance of several distinctive practices involved in this process that include posters, community history, queer zines, community histories, and historical documentation, among others, notably through digital media or archived across network media and online settings today. In parallel to Halberstam, it could be argued how The Chinky Homo Project theorizes the practices of archiving with reference to this new digital and participatory method. Furthermore, in this process, it also extends a nuanced understanding of archives as spatial documentation curated to sustain a sense of communal belonging among these marginalized communities. The evolution and pervasiveness of digital technologies have intrinsically altered what archives are. This is fundamentally where The Chinky Homo Project could be situated.

It could be noted how the role and importance of self-acceptance remain crucial in the acceptance of one's queer identity. The Chinky Homo Project focuses on this very idea of outward expression of the self in this journey of self-acceptance. With reference to this, Lede E. Miki Pohshna (2020) states how queering "the everyday in The Chinky Homo Project is then an attempt to see and read the everyday through the eyes of queer people. Their everyday is a farrago of conflict and the mundane, yet this everyday life is significant enough in understanding queer experiences" (Café Dissensus). The everyday dynamics of the queer identities documented here are reflective of the scholarship surrounding the nontraditional forms of resistance in everyday life, as opposed to the often-polarised construction of organised resistance. Some of the archives document queer subjectivities in search of a community, resulting in activism of different sorts; others speak of shifting from the closet into the obscurity of urban existence. It could be, however, noted that these changes stem from a very understanding of these politics of everyday as acts of resistance, which play a crucial role in shaping not merely one's creative expression but also their individual conviction of queer identity. Digital cultures representing minority identities, like The Chinky Homo Project where the democratisation of NER's queer people and their sense of nostalgia, belongingness, and solidarity remain the fundamental basis of its motivation, the crucial question that emerges here is not how they delve into this archival practice. But rather, in what manner do they redefine the everyday archiving practices, where identities significantly lie at the intersection of memory, technology, and affective virtual solidarities? While these digital archives might not be a part of what is formally considered as mainstream national or international archives, they essentially provide a counter-narrative on emerging archiving practices sustaining minority identities, both shared and individual.

## Conclusion:

In considering the ways archives produce relational-communal minority conversations[13], it is important to begin by thinking about how their identities are implicated in their hometowns in NER, and thereby, in turn, their personal uncritical autobiography becomes shared collective communal narratives of growth and survival. Representation remains crucial to the expression of identity. Representations—of both socialized body and identity—understood

[13] "Observed conversations," as mentioned by Pavel Sagolsem in his interview. Refer to the excerpt from the interview with Pavel Sagolsem, co-founder of The Chinky Homo Project, 2022. [Goswami, Nilakshi (2021, January 29). Personal Communication with Pavel Sagolsem (Interview on Zoom)].

as confessional in a post-structuralist framework[14]. Sally Munt (2002) observes "confession" as a persistent practice that renders the subject "visible and plausible to itself, and to others" (18). This form of collective identity is not just built on what Appadurai (2003) states as the "will to archive" but is further constructed on a sense of shared struggle and a nostalgic past that is distinctively created through digital engagement, interactive participation, and co-creative practices within the digital platforms, like reading and commenting, and in turn, transmuting the world of the virtual into a real world of minority community engagement. This, in turn, adds to this ongoing "observed conversation," a dialogue in a fragmented, non-linear fashion that portrays an individual, personalized, and collective community history.

With a specific reference to The Chinky Homo Project as a case study, the chapter has, thereby, examined how far the digital spaces enable the possibility of an alternative space for navigation of self-acceptance and expression of one's sense of identity and shared belongingness where one could be "(un) comfortably queer"[15]. Considering the particular implications of visibility/invisibility of queer living, the study—drawn

---

14 Michel Foucault discusses the idea of confession, especially the way it was developed on sex. In particular, the third section of the book, Scientia Sexualis, offers significant insight into the idea of confession has been often perceived as a way to procure the truth. In the early discourse on sex, there were many systematic blindnesses, "a refusal to see and to understand; but further . . . a refusal concerning the very thing that was brought to light and whose formulation was urgently solicited. For there can be no misunderstanding that is not based on a fundamental relation to truth" (Foucault 55). In the early stages of this discourse, the popular opinion was that the truth must not be revealed, so it would not have to be acknowledged. However, in the sixteenth century, during and after the Counter Reformation, there was a new push to discover the truth about sex, a truth acquired through confession. This truth acted as a form of knowledge-power - a Foucauldian term that references the power achieved through receiving a truth. Instead of being vouched for by someone else, the individual had the power to authenticate themself through the discourse of their truth. For further information, see Foucault, Michel (1990), The History of Sexuality, Volume 1, Vintage Books.

15 Refer to the title of the paper.

from paradigmatic theoretical structures of gender studies, along with interviews and digital archival research—aimed at providing a grounded and contextualized account of queer lives of Northeastern lived with and expressed through digital media in a context characterized as detrimental to the mental well-being of the queer. The analytical thrust of this research has been to provide a renewed outlook into how the notion of queer identity and queer embodiment in NER and its purpose and relationship to the archive has shifted over time.

## References:


1. Ahmed, Sara (2006). Orientations: Toward a queer phenomenology. GLQ, 12(4), 543–574. doi: https://doi.org/10.1215/10642684-2006-002, accessed 6 June 2018.
2. Alcoff, Linda Martín (2005). Visible identities: Race, gender, and the self. Oxford University Press.
3. Appadurai, Arjun (2003). Archive and aspiration. In Brouwer J and Mulder A (Eds), Information Is Alive. Rotterdam (pp. 14–25). V2_Publishing and NAI Publishers
4. Baruah, Sanjib (2020). In the Name of the Nation: India and its Northeast. Stanford University Press.
5. D'Emilio, John (1983). Sexual politics, sexual communities: The making of a homosexual minority in the United States, 1940–1970. University of Chicago Press.
6. Daivdson, Kumam, and Pavel Sagolsem (2018). The Chinky Homo Project. https://thechinkyhomoproject.wordpress.com/
7. Darsey, James (1991). From 'gay is good' to the scourge of AIDS: The evolution of gay liberation rhetoric, 1977–1990. Communication Studies, 42 (1), 43–66. doi: https://doi.org/10.1080/10510979109368320, accessed 6 June 2018.
8. Foucault, Michel (1990). The History of Sexuality. Vintage Books.
9. Goswami, Nilakshi (2018). Retracing the Discourse of Referential Truth in Claude Cahun and Alison Bechdel's Visual Narratives. In Aparna Lanjewar Bose (Ed.), Writing Them(Selves): Women's Autobiographies Around the World (1st ed., pp. 101-119). Routledge.
10. Halberstam, Jack (2008). What's that smell? Queer temporalities and subcultural lives. In Driver S (Ed.), Queer Youth Cultures. (pp. 27–50). SUNY Press.
11. Hanhardt, Christina B (2013). Safe space: Gay neighborhood history and the politics of violence. Duke University Press.

12. Munt, Sally (2002) Framing intelligibility, identity, and selfhood: a reconsideration of spatio-temporal models. Reconstruction, 2 (3).
13. Nanda, Serena (1999). Neither Man nor Woman: The Hijras of India. Wadsworth Pub. Co.
14. Peletz, Michael G (2009). Gender Pluralism: Southeast Asia Since Early Modern Times. Routledge.
15. Pohshna, Lede E Miki (2020). "Queering the Everyday: North East India and its Queer experiences." Café Dissensus.
16. Rao, Rahul (2020). Out of Time: The Queer Politics of Postcoloniality. Oxford University Press.
17. Shapiro, Eve (2004). Transcending barriers: Transgender organizing on the Internet. Journal of Gay & Lesbian Social Services, 16 (4), 165–179. doi: https://doi.org/10.1300/J041v16n03_11
18. Singh, Vijaita (2021, April 12). Northeast citizens faced racial discrimination amid COVID-19 outbreak, says govt. study. The Hindu.
19. Whittle, Stephen (1998). The trans-cyberian mail way. Social & Legal Studies, 7(3), 389–408. doi: https://doi.org/10.1177/096466399800700304, accessed 6 June 2018.

Unit 3

# Homophobia and Cultural Sensibility in Northeast

# Looking beyond the Binaries: Examining Homophobia in a middle-class Assamese Community in a Mofussil town

**Namami Sharma**

## Abstract:

The discussion on gender and sexuality has gained ground in Assam in recent times. The youth has come out openly in support of the LGBTQIA+ movement. It is widely seen that these voices belong largely to the urban young people. However, the perception of queer identities among the wider population of Assam is yet to be traced. The article examines the assumption of existing homophobia among the members of the Assamese community. It would further examine the factors behind the formation of such perceptions. An enquiry on the influence of culture and religiosity will be specifically made to understand the construction of the perceptions. The article would consider primary information collected from purposely selected respondents. This information would be analysed in the backdrop of the emerging discourse on gender and sexuality. The narratives from the respondents would be examined further to find strategies in normalizing the non-binary gender identities.

**Keywords:** *Homophobia, perceptions, gender, sexuality, Identity*

## Introduction:

While delivering the landmark verdict decriminalizing homosexuality and upholding fundamental rights of the LGBTQ community, then Chief Justice of India Dipak Misra quoted Goethe's, *"I am what I am, so take me as I am"*. As the gender discourse is gaining momentum, it is seen to be accommodating the non- binary gender identities very well. The discourse is giving space to the various gender identities and sexualities across the spectrum.

One emerging space to dialogue, express and inspire is the pride walks. The pride movement in the last decade has gained ground in northeast India as well, with its first pride march conducted in Guwahati in the year 2014. The city witnessed the constant effort to normalise and include the non-binary identities. It has further been able to bring in a change in the way cisgendered heterosexual people look at their non-binary identities. It is seen that the allies are growing in number, and this gives us a beacon of hope. "Pride (walks) is the space of the urban elite", opined one acquaintance. I realized that pride indeed has been occupying spaces only in cosmopolitan cities on examining this comment. It is seen that the urban people have been behind creating this space and taking it forwards. I would leap and make a hypothesis that the pride movement through its various activities has the potential to sensitize people and increase the level of awareness among the heterosexual population, thus reducing homophobia. This makes me question the 'inclusivity' and outreach of the pride movement. Do we see non-binary identities from rural areas participate or be a part of the pride march? Is pride able to reach out to the people on the margins? I am tempted to answer affirmation because as I write this article pride walks have been organized in Jorhat, a small township in upper Assam. Planning has been going on to organize one in Tezpur, yet another small town in central Assam. We do see a section of queer identities come in from rural areas but the outreach is yet to be ascertained. As the popular media has started to demonstrate non-binary identities and homosexuality in certain ways, sometimes even flawed, has it been able to change the attitude and perspective of the cis heterosexual people from the Mofussil towns and rural areas of the country? Will the spaces created by the movement remain unreachable or inaccessible to the individuals in the non-urban localities? When I talk about inclusion, are older people identifying with alternative sexualities also included in the movement?

In this article, I am examining homophobia across different age groups in the small town of Assam, a state in the northeastern part of India. I would operationalise homophobia as per the definition of George Weinberg (1972) which implied the negative attitudes toward homosexuality. The findings would help us understand the outreach and impact of the pride and would also give us a way forward.

## Methodology:

With the above questions in the backdrop, I started my enquiry. I chose a small town in the upper Assam valley which is a historic and cultural seat of the Ahom kings. I interacted with people, both men and women, and tried to trigger a discussion on gender identities, sexual orientation and homosexuality in particular. I interacted with 33 respondents. Barring a few occasions of awkward silence, diverted gaze and change of topics, most discussions were good. The discussions were both held with single respondents and a group of 2-3. It was also seen that the discussion could die out if it's a mixed group of both male and female members. The awkward silences would emanate if the term 'sex' or 'sexuality' is used.

The conversations were analysed around key statements that entered the discussions. These key statements were mostly expressed at the beginning of the discussion. The question to trigger the discussion was common to all, which was, "How do you feel about homosexuals?". In some cases, I referred to popular Hindi films to steer the discussion on the topic. I came across both calm and embarrassed dispositions. From each discussion, a few statements reflecting the perception of homosexuals were overarching across the groups. I have taken these statements and analysed the same drawing from existing literature.

### "Homosexuality is an illness. They need treatment"

One of the earliest biased statements against homosexuals, this was still found common among the responses. This statement was one of the most common responses from the age group 45 and above. The responses attributed homosexuality to an illness. The respondents sympathized with homosexuals and opined that they need treatment. When asked, which specialist could treat a homosexual, the responses varied from 'God' to mental health specialists. One respondent who was aware of the mental health discourse in contemporary times believed that through counselling homosexuality can be cured. "One needs to counsel them and show them the reality". This statement comes from respondents who take the role of the guardian of culture, family and society. Homosexuality is perceived as an abnormal trait in human beings.

Clubbing homosexuals with mental health patients was not an unusual phenomenon before the 1970s. However, in the 1970s, scholars carried out multiple studies to establish the absence of any relationship between homosexuality and mental illness (Ross, Paulsen, & Stalstrom, 1988). (Green, 1972) believed homosexuality was a case of arbitrary definition where psychiatry used the consensus among society and psychiatrists to impose the status of the disorder. Green had questioned whether a homosexual's psychological functioning is healthy or normal. A classified mental illness has a set of symptoms which is universally seen in all patients suffering from that particular illness. Green contended this assumption based on the above premise. If homosexuality is a disorder or illness then, all homosexuals must exhibit the same symptoms. Even if a few homosexuals exhibit psychological adjustments within the normal range, Green contends that homosexuality can never be a disorder or an illness.

There have been several studies which argue and establish that homosexuality is not a psychological illness. Still, a newspaper in the year 2019 reported the opinions of a section of educated youth who suggested that homosexuality is indeed an illness and can be cured through medicine.

### 'Poor parents'

Discussion with a few respondents who were retired from their professional life had deep-felt sympathy for the parents of homosexuals. They did not express any disgust or fear but blamed it on the ill fate of the parents. "*I feel so sad for the parents.*" Was a common statement. The feeling of sympathy emanated out of anonacceptance of homosexuality. It was noted that the sympathy for the parents of homosexuals was on two grounds. One, there would not be successive generations to carry on the lineage of the family and two, challenges in facing the social stigma. The statement relied heavily on the heteronormative society centering around reproduction and progeny. "*How would the family survive*?" was another opinion often uttered during the discussions.

The expression of sympathy also reflected the othering of the community. The respondents never took into account the consideration that their family members may also have an orientation towards the same sex. They vehemently denied that there could be homosexuals in their immediate families which again reflected the stigma and deep-rooted phobia.

A study was carried out in Germany looking into the acceptance of fathers of their homosexual children. The study was conducted with fathers between 28 to 60 years of age. It was found that fathers with a strong masculine orientation i.e. adhering to qualities like assertiveness, independence, physical strength etc.) are more likely to reject children who come out as gay or lesbian. This rejection stems from the father's homophobic distress he may go through in facing society. (Kranz, 2021).

A few respondents pointed out parenting 'flaws' leading to children becoming homosexuals. This implies that the parents are blamed for the sexual orientation of the children, and this further adds to the latter taking a defensive stance. Studies have shown that physical abuse by a male parent or a distanced father and unhappy childhood could be a common occurrence amongst homosexual men but is not established as the sole causal reason.

Respondents also misunderstood the difference between gay men with feminine expressions with intersex individuals. I felt that the respondents thought these individuals were 'hijras' who would eventually break away from families and take up begging as an option. They owed these ideas to the popular depiction of intersex individuals in Bollywood movies.

Same-sex relationships were seen as a hindrance to procreation and thus were stigmatized and marginalized to discourage the same. The assertion of the typically masculine traits like anger, aggression, dominance, assertiveness, physical strength, etc. or typically feminine traits like submissiveness, shy, meek, soft-spoken, etc. in the families and the larger society make it uncomfortable for children to express and parents to accept. The assertions are reiterated by popular media, cultural norms, traditions, etc.

## "Do not Understand the range"

Young adults, between the age of 20-and 27, seemed confused about the difference between the non-binary gender identities. "*I get conceptually confused between the terms. Are the intersex and hijras the same*? ...*Are all women who look like 'men' lesbians*?" were a few key questions that were asked in different forms. These respondents were young adults who were willing to understand and empathise with the non-binary genders and sexualities. They felt the need to have an equal emancipated society where non-binary gender identities are a part of the society. "*Our society should be such wherein if a biological boy wears mekhela chador and walks into the naamghor, it should not raise eyebrows*", shared one of the respondents. The empathy and the willingness to accept were reflected in their desire to have a gender-inclusive and gender diverse society. However, the same set of respondents shared that they have inadequate conceptual clarity on the different types of non-binary gender identities. " *The different alphabets represent the different identities but I don't think I have a clear understanding*", shared one respondent. The understanding is based on popular representations as well as social media handles. "*In Instagram, there are several handles belonging to non-binary couples and it has helped me accept them easily. However, the same cant be accepted from our parent's generation*", shared another respondent.

One of them gave the example of plants and animals where gender beyond the binary exists. However, their understanding lacked clarity due to which their treatment of the subject often carried prejudice. "*We know about the LGBTQ+ movement but lack conceptual clarity about the terms difference,"*, shared one of the respondents in a group discussion. Respondents also indicated that they have not yet met any individual with an alternate sexual identity or orientation. Being straight heterosexual people, they are not sure whether they would be accepted in the community of the non-binary identities. Having inclusive and integrated spaces in mofussil towns to dialogue, discuss and share could go a long way.

## "Modern age modern ideas"

A few respondents in the age group 45+ dismissed homosexuality as 'modern age ideas'. This set of respondents was insistent with their own heterosexual identity and reiterated that they have not come across any homosexual person in their life. They believed that homosexuality is a recent phenomenon and a modern idea. They felt the portrayal of homosexuals in popular media is a wrong influence.

While using the term 'modern', a trend was implied. The analogy drawn was with fashion trends that are often the flavour of a specific time. Trends come and go, and so will homosexuality. "It is becoming a fashion" is a comment given by a respondent and agreed by a few. This statement was used interchangeably with the "it's just a phase'" statement.

This statement infers that homosexuality will eventually turn into heterosexuality in the coming time. Just like any other adolescent musing, this 'phase' was attributed to hormones, popular films, popular film icons, and the 'craze' to sound or be different. Respondents also felt that children in the process of rebelling against their families or parents can get into this 'phase' with 'such' ideas only to later come out and be 'normal'. This statement is also heavy with hope with a bit of cynicism. The hope is that the person will realise and come out of the trend with age.

The term homosexuality was coined in the late 19$^{th}$ century by Karoly Maria Benkert (Stanford Encyclopedia of Philosophy, 2020). However, same-sex romance and sex have been a subject of deliberations since the time of ancient Greeks. Homosexuality was a subject of scholarly discussions and writings but was looked at as an exception. Getting attracted to men was also seen as a sign of masculinity. Heroic figures in Greek Myths and mythologies have often mentioned same-sex exploits. However, this was also centred around status. Men of higher standing could have a relationship with younger men belonging to a lower status and not vice-versa. The relationships have a dominant and a submissive partner as was the norm in heterosexual relationships. (Plato, 1981)

Michel Foucault in his landmark work "History of Sexuality" suggests that homosexuality is just a matter of preference which may be nothing more than taste or practice with no deeper roots to the soul for which there is a quest to understand. (Thorp, 1992). This also establishes that homosexuality is not a modern idea. It has always been there in society, in dire need of the right words and the right space to get articulated.

## "It's self-inflicting and thus can be avoided and reversed"

Group discussions with a few respondents (30+ years old) elicited that homosexuality is not by birth but is an adopted trait. It is interesting to note that this discussion took place with a set of respondents who were well aware of the alternative sexualities and had deliberated on the issue in the past. The respondents suggested that the coping strategy is a defence mechanism to deal with certain incidents that may have happened in childhood. The respondents referred to an episode of "Satyameva Jayate", a weekly television talk series made on various social issues. This particular episode was on "Child sexual abuse" (CSA) wherein, one participant had been a victim of sodomy and eventually discovered his orientation to be gay. They referred to a confused sexual identity arising out of CSA.

It was also pointed out that children who have experienced domestic violence often 'develop' alternative sexuality. It was suggested that witnessing a bad experience with heterosexual parents, may lead to disillusionment towards conventional marriages. They also gave a reference to homosexual persons who had troubled relationships with /her parent/s. Homosexuality was seen as a coping strategy by this group of respondents. Again, they believed that it can be avoided and reversed with proper counselling and empathetic treatment.

Let us see what the existing literature speaks on this front. Research says that there is a link between child sexual abuse and sexual orientation (Yin Xu, 2015). It was found that the heterosexual and non-heterosexual men who were not conforming to the gender they were born into, had a greater likelihood of being abused in their childhood as compared to their gender-conforming counterparts. Epidemiological studies establish a positive association between childhood maltreatment and alternative sexual orientation in adulthood(HL Corliss, 2002; TL Hughes, 2000). Results from several studies suggest that from half to all of the increased prevalence of childhood sexual abuse experienced by individuals with alternative sexualities compared with heterosexuals "may be due to the effects of sexual abuse on sexual orientation, possibly through previously proposed pathways: (1) abuse of boys perpetrated by men causes boys to believe they are gay; (2) abuse of girls by men leads them to be averse to sexual relationships with men; (3) abuse survivors may feel stigmatized and different from others and may, therefore, be more willing to behave in ways that are socially stigmatized, including acknowledging same-sex attraction or having same-sex partners". (Saewyc EM, 2006).

Thus it appears that the speculation on the association between child sexual abuse and homosexuality may have certain pieces of evidence, especially in the case of gay men. However, none of the studies suggested that through counselling, it could be reversed. Also, not all cases of alternative sexualities can be routed to CSA.

### "Lesbians are fine but gay men are disgusting"

Within the social hierarchy of sexual orientation, heteronormativity serves as the dominant force. Violation of this force elicits negative emotions amongst the heterosexual population. It is interesting to see that prejudice and bias are more toward gay men than towards lesbians. As I interacted with young adults, I found a difference in the attitude toward gay men and lesbians. The broader emotion was 'unacceptance' and 'bias'. However, the extent of the negative emotion varied between gay men and lesbians. (Ray & Parkhill, 2021).

The above was one of the common statements I came across during my interactions with young adult men. Young adult women too found gay men less likeable than lesbians. This statement reflects homophobia amongst the heterosexual population for gay men while also upholding a fantasy for lesbians. The idea of two women making love is pictured as a scene of erotica and sensuousness by men while the same men find the idea of two men making love 'disgusting'. A survey was carried out in the United States in the year 1997 to understand how heterosexuals think about gay men and lesbians. The survey also included the intersectionality of race. The interviews were done with 976 White and 479 Black individuals. The findings showed favourable attitudes of men and women towards lesbians compared to gay men. The study suggested possible gender differences in the cognitive organization of heterosexuals' attitudes towards gay men and lesbians. (Herek & Capitanio, 1999).

In cinema, there are many examples of erotic depictions of lesbian relationships. The same is not seen in the case of gay men. The beauty of the feminine is reflected in lesbian depiction while the same is not commonly seen in the case of gay men.

Also, usually, strength is associated with masculinity while femininity exudes delicacy, weakness, and submissiveness. The traits are socially constructed around the two genders and the gender performances affirm the same. A butch woman showing masculine gender traits may come across as a strong empowered woman while a man with feminine traits may be judged as a meek man thus eliciting a stronger stigma.

**"Homosexuality is the new fad and people act like one just to come across as interesting and different"**

As the pride movement is gaining ground in Assam, young people are finding the right vocabulary and platforms to come out and express themselves. I interacted with conscious and aware young adults who called themselves allies of the community but were also sceptical of certain members. " *I support the LGBTQIA+ individuals with all my heart but I detest the fake ones*", shared a 29 years old girl. On further probe, she explained what she meant by 'fake ones'. She referred to women who used to be feminine and changed their gender expression overnight. She felt that they do it under the influence of media and peers. She felt that such individuals dilute the cause of the 'real community members. *"I feel for the 'natural ones', but many are just following the 'trend"*, she added. The discussion with the respondents mentioned certain individuals known to me and I realized that all the references were women who came out as lesbians. It was implied that women coming out as a lesbian was the fad that was referred to as opposed to gay men. They believed that the stigma for gay men is relatively higher compared to lesbian words, lesbian took it as a fad to belong to the community.

The respondents who affirmed this statement were not homophobic but were skeptical of the fad that is catching up. They are allies and are out there in spirit for the community and the cause. As the movement is gaining ground and the community members are getting attention on social media, the number of people coming out is also increasing. The increase in numbers strengthens the movement and gives voice to the members. Gender and sexuality are not static but are transient. Having said that, it may also be only normal for a person to discover her sexuality overnight. I felt that the sceptics are only a small distance away from the phobics. They do not harbour hatred but are dismissive.

## Conclusion:

The article began by examining certain questions on homosexuality and homophobia. Through the followed methodology, the key statements reflective of the discussions were drawn and analysed. It was seen that the small towns still harboured the orthodox outlook and homophobic sentiments on the fact of a structured heteronormative society. Age-oldnotions of equating homosexuality with mental illness or dismissing it as a passing trend are still very prevalent. The recognition of homosexuals with due dignity is yet to be achieved. The younger generation who are exposed to social media and other media platforms are aware of the community and the movement. Since the movement is providing a free liberated space for sexual expression, the young adults find it attractive. It will be premature to say if this attraction would also lead to the acceptance of alternative sexualities in the mainstream. The beacon of hope lies in the fact that this generation is open to ideas and it is an indicator that it is high time the movement touches the small towns and rural areas. It must address the intersectionalities within society. The lower caste gay man in the village or the minority community lesbian must find an equal space within the movement. It should venture out of the boundaries of the urban educated elite and enter into the rural areas.

It is very important to include and increase the allies of the movement. More allies from all walks of life would give voice to the community members languishing on the margins of society. Strategic interventions like support spaces for the LGBTQIA+ community members with the active participation of the allies need to be created. Pride walks must be organized in all parts of northeast India and must be endorsed by prominent people of the society. All-inclusive pride walks would give visibility and belongingness to the movement.

## References:


1. Kranz, D. (2021). Associations Between Fathers' Masculinity Orientation and Anticipated Reaction Toward Their Child's Coming Out. *Frontiers in Psychology*.
2. *Stanford Encyclopedia of Philosophy*. (2020, April 28). Retrieved from Plato stanford edu: https://plato.stanford.edu/entries/homosexuality/#Bib
3. Plato. (1981). *The Symposium*. Penguin.

4. Thorp, J. (1992). Social Construction of Homosexuality. *Phoenix*, 54-61.
5. Yin Xu, Y. Z. (2015). Does Sexual Orientation Precede Childhood Sexual Abuse? Childhood Gender Nonconformity as a Risk Factor and Instrumental Variable Analysis. *Sexual Abuse*.
6. HL Corliss, S. C. (2002). Reports of parental maltreatment during childhood in a United States population-based survey of homosexual, bisexual, and heterosexual adults. *Child Abuse and Neglect*.
7. TL Hughes, A. H. (2000). Comparing lesbians' and heterosexual women's mental health: A multi-site survey. *Journal of Gay & Lesbian Social Services.*
8. Saewyc EM, S. C. (2006). Hazards of stigma: The sexual and physical abuse of gay, lesbian, and bisexual adolescents in the United States and Canada. *Child Welfare.*
9. Ray, T. N., & Parkhill, M. R. (2021). Heteronormativity, Disgust Sensitivity, and Hostile Attitudes toward Gay Men: Potential Mechanisms to Maintain Social Hierarchies. *Sex role*.
10. Herek , G. M., & Capitanio, J. P. (1999). Sex Differences in How Heterosexuals Think about Lesbians and Gay Men: Evidence from Survey Context Effects. *The Journal of Sex Research*.
11. Green, R. (1972). Homosexuality as a mental illness. *International Journal of Psychiatry.*
12. Ross, M. W., Paulsen, J. A., & Stalstrom, O. W. (1988). Homosexuality and Mental Health: a cross cultural review. *Journal of Homosexuality*.

# Gender Obscurity and Homophobia in Northeast India

**Deepshikha Carpenter**

## Abstract:

The binary of sex- gender debate is no longer the norm of the society due to the social movement of LGBTQIA+ community across the world and recently in North East India. It is mostly the Transgender persons who are perceived to be discriminated as portrayed; whereas the 'others' too who maintain different sexual orientation suffer from homophobia and victimization. This paper is looking into exploring the stigmatization and domestic violence faced by persons with different sexual orientation, gender identity, and expression through the lens of intersectionality and cycle of violence approach. It shall probe through the in-depth narratives of queer persons to define the current crisis faced in their lives and explore the helplessness in their day-to-day activities.

**Key words:** *Northeast India, Homophobia, LGBTQIA+, Domestic Violence*

## Introduction:

Individual draws a sense of own identity from the primary members, peers and that identity becomes a sense of influence through personal, social relationships and institutions. The difference in one's identity is perceived from the gender role one plays in the society. In Indian society, heterosexuality is seen as a common phenomenon and preferred sexual orientation in public space. Lauretis (1991) defines heterosexuality as the benchmark of sexuality formation. Although culturally homosexuality is visible in architectural and religious sources; homosexuality is not considered to be an 'approved' form of sexuality; it promotes homophobia among society on the grounds of morality. It is the Heteronormativity that prevails in any type of society and is institutionally imposed on the sections that do not conform to gender binary or questions its nature. De Lauratris (1991) Gay men and women may express solidarity with one another, and the biggest help is giving to each other is recognition of the extent and nature of different context and sympathy that one gives to another to liberate. It is to come out of the various structural stigmatizations that they suffer. If the person is 'misaligned' in the aspect of social norm, the person is considered as a deviant. The situation brings in phobic oppressions to any persons who do not support the binary notion of gender. They undergo acts of prejudices such as disregarding their economic and cultural status in society to acts of murders (Bettcher, 2009) Gay people are often subjected to anti-homosexual attitudes of families and their communities (Drescher, 1998; Drescher et al., 2004).

The recent judgment of Section 377, Indian Penal Code (IPC) is argued against homogeneous views of 'public morality'. A coalition group 'Voices Against 377' which involves organizations such as Nirantar, Saheli, Jagori, Amnesty International India, CREA, Haq, PRISM, Nigah Media Collective, Partners for Law in Development, Anjuman, Breakthrough, Sama and TARSHI have uninterruptedly fought to fight for freedom, dignity and life for the homosexual relationships.

The role of civil societies and NGOs' are massive in India and they have a collective representation in holding queer parade or pride walk and since 2014 they are an integral part of North East India especially Assam.

## Sexuality orientation personal versus public:

Sedgwick's Epistemology of the Closet (2008) defines sexuality to be dependent on an individual's romantic partner; one makes that dependent on how thoughts are shaped where homosexuality

is gendered into masculine and feminine. It is a matter of choice not imposition where society plays the vivid role as an agent of social control and homosexuality is perceived as a form of deviance. Article 21 of the Indian Constitution advocates the right to privacy whereas in reality the gay community is hunted down for practicing the same sexual orientation. However, the Right to Privacy has been contested through the Section 377 IPC on sexual orientation. Individual's sexual orientation is always under public surveillance due to non-recognition and non- acceptance of homosexual relationships. It is the prevalence of dominance and hegemonic Heteronormativity to an extent that Kimmel (1998) defines, 'throughout history hegemonic masculinity was created (heterosexual, white, and Christian) and a subordinate masculinity (all the others) that presented a contrast related to race, ethnicity, sexuality, and origin'. History has portrayed a dominant form of sexuality which is contested and debated through right based ideology and identity discourse.

According to Berlant & Warner (1998), heteronormativity is a form of power and control that applies pressure to both straight and gay individuals, through institutional arrangements and accepted social norms. It is the state that targets LGBT rights claims as hostile (Bosia 2014). It is the state homophobia that is changed through case studies and LGBT organizations although in a weaker position act in cooperation with inter-governmental institutions as they have a better understanding of local context (Weiss and Bosia 2013). Hence inclusion of people with various sexual orientations is necessary in influencing government policies and claiming the space as equal.

## Objective and Methodology:

This article highlights the struggle of gay men (MSM) who shared their experience through two case studies and interpreted them as narratives. The major limitation that research found was that gay community was small and 'in the closet'; they did not want to be named or their experience being brought out due to their struggle of everyday emotions. Heterosexism condemns homosexuality morally that includes homophobia which leads to concealing different aspects of their living. Flyvbjerg (2011, p.301) shares usage of case study in the research, that does not mean the selection of a method, but rather a selection of what will be explored. Constructive Social Work seeks to open up alternative possibilities where people are excluded by their own stories; how they have understood or experienced how the world deal with them. It is trying to build on the positives in people's lives and experience (Payne, 2005).

## Case Study I

*Background*

D is aged 51 years and is a director by profession. He has a strong educational and financial background. He did his schooling from Don Bosco, Guwahati and completed his Masters from Pune University. His mom was a teacher and father was a superintendent of Assam Tea Stock. His parents died very young. One year apart from each other. D has a sister and brother-in-law with whom he shares a strong bond.

As a child, D was shy, soft spoken and lonely. He liked playing with dolls and doll house. He played the character of Parbati, Usha and Chitralekha whenever there was dramatics involved. He was often referred to as 'cute', 'adorable'. He was never engaged in football and cricket matches with people of his age in childhood. He was never a cross-dresser however, fond of traditional Assamese attire Muga Mekhala Chador worn by a female.

D's first exposure to expression of his feelings was through his cousin with whom he had an affair. He was his aunt's son. He came from Shillong. D confessed, 'My love relationship' worked for eight long years which was friendly in nature. He was a smart and smooth talker. He had an event management firm. His first interaction with the gay community started in Pune. D mentioned, 'Gay men are born gay. It is not a sudden realization whenever a boy shows interest in cooking, stitching etc.....it is not that he shall be of help to his wife in future. But the boy is actually gay Man having Sex with Man (MSM)'.

*Social Interaction and Communication*

During the period of 1991 to 1995, people used to communicate as a group to hang out in public parks such as Fancy Bazar, Nehru Park and Dighali Pukhuri. It used to be a close intimate group. D narrated 'In the evening meetings on Saturday and Sunday, cricketers, footballers and other community members used to come. We used to party a lot'. Interaction in specific spaces helped the community to thrive socially without adding into any kind of judgements.

*Relationships and Commitment*

D spoke relentlessly about the relationships. 'I have spent 13 years in Delhi. I had a strong steady relationship for 16 years with V. He wanted to get married to me. Then in 2014, G came into my life. He was just 22. He was 23 years younger than me. He was my son, my lover and my friend. It was out of this world. He was a very good lyricist. I lost him due to his illness and I am not able to get over the grief of losing him'. As the community is very small, finding a suitable partner with similar interests becomes very difficult. It leads to loneliness.

*Homophobia and violence*

Talking about relationships, D confessed, 'in my first relationship I behaved like an immature girlfriend. My partner was abusive and used to hit me with his belt. He cheated on me when we were very clear that I liked straight men. But with G it was more mature. He was attached. I did not have male friends but there was acceptance among girls. In Delhi I met a model and I had a second relationship. We continued for six years. There was a constant struggle to have a proper relationship and home and kind of bonding with whom I can have my emotional needs fulfilled. After G has gone, there is a lot of loneliness. I accepted that he got married. He had a wife. But I was very attached to him.'

Violence is a common phenomenon in heterosexual relationships. It can also be perceived among gay community due to the struggle of societal and individual needs.

*Performativity, Closet and Exploitation*

D had a gait which was not accepted by others. 'I used to be tagged as '*maiki*' (effeminate). D had a lot of guts before coming out. He said, 'I thank God. Why I think I was ahead of my time. People have become more knowledgeable now. Young boys and girls are more acceptable. People have accepted each other. There is a flourishing community of gay men from professions such as journalism, actors, make-up artists and so on.

Talking about his place of work, 'In Delhi, there is a lot of exploitation physically, emotionally, mentally among the gay community. They fall back to friends, and doctors for support. There is marriage among the gay community too. Married men do not tell their wives about their relationship as it might be offending and affecting their marital relationship'. Talking about the thriving community of transgender and cross- dressing, 'the people who come from small towns are confused with their sexual and gender orientation. Gays are not transgender. But the transgender person goes through hormonal therapy, counselling and surgery; both hormonal therapy and operation. They like wearing lipstick and make-up. I am a man who likes men. So many gays have relations. Even if I get married, my orientation will be toward men. More gays are coming out. If you are independent and make a mark, everything falls into place. A strong professional identity helps to survive among the larger community'.

In situations of exploitation, 'it appears that sometimes those who would oppress others have been oppressed themselves, and we can have some compassion for them too; they may be critical of others because they cannot accept themselves'.

Exploitation and homophobia should be recognized so there is no abuse. As the LGBTQIA+ community is growing; solidarity is very important to negotiate spaces in the social realm.

## Case 2

*Background*

P, dance teacher is Aged 35 years. He is a Dance teacher in India in semi-classical forms. He has three older sisters and one younger brother. He lost his father. He grew up having an inclination towards television musical shows such as *Chitrahaar* and *Rangoli*. He imagined himself to be a girl and wearing a scarf, dupatta and *gamusa* (Assamese towel) made him comfortable. P never preferred jackets or closed sweaters but cardigans.

*Social Interaction and Communication*

P's family, especially sisters , never discouraged him from dancing. P confessed, 'I used to go to the field wearing a bun in head, weave clothes, and do all the work, washing, cleaning, and cooking. I used to keep the home very clean. When I saw theatre, I used to like going to workshops. I saw it gave scope and opportunity to economically challenged people. Out of 100 children, only 20 belong to rich families. So I wanted a source of income. In 2004, I joined a theatre company with reputed theatre artists. I could send money home of around Rs 3000 to 4000 per month. It gave me the satisfaction of being a contributing member of my family. Family members felt that theatre was a good source of income.

Theatre was the right prospect for P and it gave him a tremendous opportunity to work on his passion for performance and earn at the same time. It gave him exposure to meet socially and culturally renowned personalities and increased his confidence level. P is respected in his community for being an exemplary artist.

*Relationships and Commitments*

P spoke about his relationships. During the theatre days, 'I had fallen in love with a boy and I was in a relationship. The boy was the hero in the theatre. Initially, I did not like the boy. One day, he confessed that he liked me a lot. I was 20 years old at that time. My financial condition was not good. So, I was involved in theatre. Through theatre, I had my source of employment. And I liked dancing too. I became a dance teacher. My heart always felt like a female. No one knows in the family that I am oriented towards men. My family wants me to get married'.

P preferred men as partners as he felt his heart was of a female. However due to societal commitment and family responsibility; P wants to enter into marriage.

*Homophobia and violence*

P talked about the negative experiences. "Men do not want to talk to me when I am alone. Young boys come and interact but older men and my friends hesitate. They say insulting words about me. I have faced more discrimination from men. Women have accepted me. Among men, it is only about physical intimacy. Some married men come for entertainment purposes bringing a packet of biscuits or eatables to have sex, but I do not allow it, although there is a strong sense of physical attraction. Some friends have fixed partners. However, most of them do not have permanent partners. Through an NGO, P has been benefited immensely and he gives awareness about HIV/AIDS. P's gay friends are married and settled with opposite sex partners. They have a family and responsibility as they say it.

*Performativity, Closet and Exploitation*

For P, wearing a saree is an expression of feeling happy and liberated. 'I do not get the freedom to be me sometimes. If I get even Rs 10, I keep buying nail polish, bangles etc. Till the age 25, I was like this dressing up for myself. Now, I have to wear shirts and jackets. My father said that I was neither male nor female. He threw objects at me. I did not have acceptance from his side. Now I am aware that there can be sex change operations but I am 35 years now and my age does not permit it. I do not want to be disabled through these operations. I am planning to get married. My heart is like a woman although I look like a man. Therefore, my fiancé knows that I understand a woman's heart and with all my past baggage she is ready to marry me'.

P has expressed honesty about his past life experience to his fiancé. It is encouraging and brave on his part to do so. Rightly, P is unafraid and ready to settle with his new life.

*Intersectionality of Gender and Class*

Butler (1999) in 'Gender Trouble' speaks about how the truth of self is obtained through acting and portraying reality. Gender performativity is a strategy of resistance resisting the binary of feminine and masculine. And both of the case studies reflect that one's sexuality is also influenced by factors of social status particularly class. D belonged to an affluent background and had freedom to join one's vocation or profession without any second thought or opinion whereas P got into theatre in order to take care of his family needs . The idea of maleness in both the narratives is practiced through the cultural dynamics that one is exposed to that leads a male to be a male and might create a pressure to get into a heterogeneous relationship for marriage.

*Cycle of Violence and Homophobia*

Both the cases reflect violence and exploitation, and they were resilient to overcome them in course of time. According to Meyer (2012), LGBT people experience all forms of anti-queer violence in different ways depending on their social position. Evidence from research also suggest gay men and lesbian suffer from more mental health problems such as substance use disorder, suicide, affective disorders (Cochran, 2001; Sandfort, de Graaf, Bijl & Schnabel, 2001). LGBTQIA+ community faces stigma, prejudice and discrimination that creates a stressful social environment leading to mental health problems. There is hiding and concealing, internalized homophobia, expectation of rejection, experience of uncalled events (Meyer, 2007; Allison 1998). In a study conducted by UN Women (2013) to look into men's attitude to homophobia or acceptance of diversity in sexual orientation; it was found out that men who would never have gay friend ranged from 21% in Brazil, 29% in Chili, Mexico at 46% and a high proportion of men nearly 89% in India had homophobic attitude. These showed developing economies had attitudinal differences in preference of same sex relationships. It was found that young men are less likely to hold homophobic attitudes, which is a welcome change.

The "gay peril" remains largely disconnected from the idea of rights. In Uganda, even while LGBT identity is still in the process of being proven as social fact through the homophobia of state actors and their allies, it is increasingly LGBT rights that are coming under attack along with the organizations that promote such rights. This is the same in the case of India as well. They are always targeted with assault and low acceptance.

## Northeast India, Gender Obscurity and Activism

With the decision of Supreme Court on 11th December, 2013 to reinstate criminality of homosexuals across India Global Day of Rage was observed on 15th December, 2013 where students, activists, and LGBTQIA community across India came united to support the community. Northeast India witnessed LGBTQIA+ community through Pride Walk organised by Xukia way back in 2014 where students across academic institutions and organizations, activists and students participated in the rally.

Anaajoree, another organization also primarily works on the issues of gender and sexuality to bridge the gap among the various populations. The Chinki Homo Project is a digital archive to create the space for representing the people of northeast and their str uggle towards queer identity. Representation of sexuality in northeast India should be marked with tolerance and equality. In Assam or other parts of India as a part of theatre or indigenous *bhaona*[1]. It is the male performer who plays the female characters whenever needed. It shows flexibility or fluidity in gender performance.

---

1 It is a Performing Art form

There is no sense of protection of the people of northeast outside the region and they are often subjected to racial profiling, lack of network and under representation of their sexual orientation. There is no strong platform to bring the community 'out of the closet'. A character that is found in the Amazon series of Patal Lok as 'Chinkie' represents the actual politics of people from the region. There is a constant struggle and anxiety to search for a place of work and so called home outside northeast India. Guwahati is a place of self-discovery and opportunity in Northeast India and it also is a potential zone for active campaigning for their rights to form a greater network for inclusion and removing homophobia. It also serves as a platform for various creative people into professions such as acting, fashion, directing and other forms of ingenious work.

## Conclusion

Over the Top (OTT) platform series and cinema such as Modern Love, Shubh Mangal Zyada Saavdhan, Beyond the Horizon, Fire and the recent Junaki Porua have incorporated relationships for the LGBTQIA+ in positive manner acceptance and inclusivity. West and Zimmerman (1987), gender roles are related to behavioral aspects of being a man or a woman which might be played out as per a prescribed format. People act out their natures either according to masculine and feminine. According to Goffman (1976), gender is a part of everyday negotiation of an individual with his/her gender role and identity. In order to reduce homophobia for the same sex relationship or rather the LGBTQIA+ community; the realization of substantive freedom is very important to facilitate decision making as well as empowerment for economic and social accessibility. Religious institutions should be based on practicing love and tolerance instead of stigmatization and exclusion. Rights should be able to be practiced by rights holders and therefore networking is mandatory not only in social media but society as a whole. Hence the role of civil society is great to be called as a movement to remove the facade of personal as political. It is to disrupt the hegemonic Heteronormativity; providing a negotiable space to remove inequality by making it a liberal choice rather than state intervention of coercion. Civil Society can provide through various electronic and social movements the choice toward collective freedom.

## Reference:


1. Allison KW. (1998). Stress and oppressed social category membership. In: Swim JK, Stangor C, (Eds.). *Prejudice: The target's perspective.* San Diego, CA: Academic Press. 145–170.
2. Berland, L & Warner, M. (1998). Sex in Public. *Critical Inquiry.* 24 (2). 547-566.
3. Bosia, M.J. (2014) Strange Fruit: Homophobia, the State, and the Politics of LGBT Rights and Capabilities, *Journal of Human Rights,* 13(3). 256-273, DOI: 10.1080/14754835.2014.919217
4. Boyce, P. (2006). Moral Ambivalence and Irregular Practices: Contextualizing Male-to-Male Sexualities in Calcutta/India. *Feminist Review, 83,* 79–98. http://www.jstor.org/stable/3874384
5. Butler, J. (1999). *Gender trouble: Feminism and the subversion of identity.* New York: Routledge.
6. Cochran, S. D. (2001). Emerging issues in research on lesbians' and gay men's mental health: Does sexual orientation really matter? *American Psychologist.* 56 :931–947.
7. DeLauretis, T. (1991). Queer Theory: Lesbian and Gay Sexualities. *A Journal of Feminist Cultural Studies.* 3(2).
8. Flyvbjerg, B. (2011). Case study. In: N. K. Denzin & Y. S. Lincoln (Eds.), The Sage Handbook of Qualitative Research (4th ed., pp. 301–316). Thousand Oaks, CA: Sage
9. Friedman, R.C. (1999). Homosexuality, psychopathology, and suicidality. Archives of General Psychiatry.56:887–888.
10. Goffman, E. (1976). Gender Display. *Studies in the Anthropology of Visual Communication.* 3
11. Kimmel, M. A. (1998). Produção simultânea de masculinidades hegemônicas e subalternas.
12. Horizontes Antropológicos, 4(9), 103-118.
13. Michael J. Bosia (2014) Strange Fruit: Homophobia, the State, and the Politics of LGBT Rights and Capabilities, *Journal of Human Rights,* 13:3, 256-273, DOI: 10.1080/14754835.2014.919217
14. Meyer, D. (2012). An Intersectional Analysis of Lesbian, Gay, Bisexual, and Transgender (LGBT) People's Evaluations of Anti-Queer Violence. *Gender & Society,* 26(6), 849–873. https://doi.org/10.1177/0891243212461299
15. Meyer I. H. (2003). Prejudice, social stress, and mental health in lesbian, gay, and bisexual populations: conceptual issues and research evidence. Psychological bulletin, 129(5), 674–697. https://doi.org/10.1037/0033-2909.129.5.674

16. Payne, M. (2005). *Modern social work theory* ($3^{rd}$ Ed. ). Palgrave Macmillan. Pp 172
17. Sandfort TG, de Graaf R, Bijl RV, Schnabel P. (2001) Same-sex sexual behavior and psychiatric disorders: Findings from the Netherlands Mental Health Survey and Incidence Study (NEMESIS) *Archives of General Psychiatry.* 58:85– 91.
18. UN Women. (December, 2013). Making Women Count. An Annual Publication on Gender and
19. Evaluation by UN Women Multi Country Office for India, Bhutan,Sri Lanka and Maldives https://www.equimundo.org/wp-content/ uploads/2015/01/ Measuring-Gender-Attitude-Using-Gender-Equitable- Men-Scale.pdf
20. Sedgwick, E. K. (2008). *Epistemology of the closet.* University of California Press.
21. West, C. & Zimmerman, D. H. (1987). Doing Gender. *Gender & Society*. 1(2)

# Lived Experiences of Gay Men in the City of Guwahati

**Prateeti Barman, Alimuddin Ahmed**


## Abstract:

Gender and sexuality have created a space in northeast India in a very mild form over the years. This paper is based on a qualitative study carried out to understand the lived experiences of the gay men in the city of Guwahati which is one of the largest cities in northeast India. Though we have gay men soliciting partners in various hotspots of the city, most of them prefer to keep their identities hidden. In that process, they are subjected to various forms of violence and abuse. Emotional isolation and social ostracism are something common which makes them even more vulnerable. The present study for the first time tries to understand the lived experiences of the gay men in the city and how far they have been able to live their lives to the fullest.


**Key words:** *Lived experiences, gay, sexuality, abuse and violence.*

## Background and Methodology:

The Guwahati city, the gateway to northeast India, has witnessed the presence of the queer community in public through the pride walk once in every year since 2014. The presence of the queer community in the city of Guwahati is bonded by well-wishers, few organizations working besides the government-funded organizations. The government-funded organizations are working in the areas of safe sex, HIV/AIDS and the local organizations are focusing and working with the queer community concerning their rights, safety and psychosocial issues.

The study started with the gay men revolving on questions of their preferred sexuality and problems they face and how do they cope in their lives due to their sexuality? A total seven participants participated in the study where snow bowling technique was used to meet the participants of the study. For data collection in

-depth interviews were conducted in a preferred location of the participants. The interview lasted for approximately one hour to two hours. The researchers ensured that privacy, dignity and self-determination of the participants were kept in mind in every stage of the study. As one of the researchers was volunteering in an organization working for the queer community in the area of HIV/ AIDS helped in approaching the participants besides social media through which one of the participants of the study was contacted. It was a voluntary participation on the part of the participants to be interviewed for the study. An informed consent was taken where objectives of the study were explained to the participants. None withdrew from the study, though, they were informed that at any given point if they felt like withdrawing from the study they could do so. To maintain the confidentiality of the participants' assumed names are used in the study.

## Findings:

### Sexuality and Identity

The first participant of the study Pranab shared that from childhood he was attracted towards boys and till now he has been having relationships with men. At the time of interview, he was in a steady relationship with his boyfriend. However, at times he gets into casual sexual relationships with others. Regarding his preference for men, Pranab said that he feels very feminine and likes masculine men. Since childhood he has been having feminine qualities and his parents have been very supportive towards him. They never tried to change him or his demeanour, in fact in his own word's parents treated him like a 'girl'. Our second participant is Prankul, a 17-year-old college goer. According to him he is a 'closet gay' as he feels that our society is not going to accept homosexuals. He prefers to keep his sexuality and identity a secret as he does not feel that society is progressive enough to accept gay or lesbians. He does not even feel any support from the queer pride which is an integral part of Guwahati city and queer community. At the time of the interview Prankul was not seeing anyone seriously, though he was in a relationship with different partners. His sexual identity developed with a man elder to him who used to follow him to his tuition. The mutual attraction made them meet regularly, watch pornographic gay movies and ended up having a sexual relationship.

Rajak, our next participant of the study, was a daily wage earner. He shared that since childhood he was attracted towards men and eventually got molested by an elderly man in his village with whom he had a relationship later on. He said that even his peers and older boys molested him when he was ten to eleven years old. While getting molested he was also exposed to gay pornographies. Rajak was brutally beaten when his sexual orientation became public in the village. His own family members were also involved in physically assaulting him. At times the feeling of rejection was so strong that he tried committing suicide twice in his native place. After these two incidents, he decided to relocate to Guwahati city where he felt there was a feeling of anonymity. However, his ordeal did not end there. As he moved to Guwahati and not keeping any relationship with his family, his family tricked him. He was summoned by his family saying that his mother was not keeping well and, in that pretext, he was married to a girl. The marriage was obviously a turbulent one and it ended with a divorce after 8 months. After the divorce, he again came back to Guwahati and since then living his life as a gay man. Our next participant Pinku preferred not to divulge his profession and he shared that he realized that he is a gay when he started having an affair with his home tutor. Though they had a relationship it was a sexual molestation in the beginning from his tutor. However, gradually he started liking it and continued their relationship. At the time of interview, he shared that he is very active in finding partners via visiting the hotspots of Guwahati city where the gay men solicit partners. He was equally active in social media for the same reason. Sharing his sexuality and identity, participants of the study Prantik said that he knew that he was attracted to boys from the age of 12 years old. However, his first sexual encounter happened after his 12th standard. in a party with his male friend when he was intoxicated. Prantik shared that he is mostly engaged with oral sex but at times his partners force him to have anal sex. Prantik said that he was a gay and would like to identify as a gay, however, he mentioned that his parents were planning to get him married to a girl.

Our next participant Mrinal is a 32-year-old NGO worker working for the gay community. He shared that he has been attracted towards boys since his teenage years and identifies himself as a gay. He prefers to have friendship and deep understanding with his partners. For him that is more important than casual sexual encounters. Shantanu, a businessman by profession was a 31-year-old man who shared his experience as a gay in the city of Guwahati. He realised his sexual orientation when he was sharing a room with a boy when he was working outside the state of Assam. They were involved for a brief period in a passionate relationship, however later on it ended on a sad note. During the interview, he shared that he is engaged with his partner who was based in upper Assam. Though Shantanu identifies himself as a gay he would not like to get involved with the organizations working for the LGBTQIA.

## Violence and Trauma

Regarding their experiences with violence and trauma out of the seven participants four of them shared that they have experienced it. Pranab sharing his part of violence and trauma said that he experienced it as a child due to his mannerisms. His headmistress openly insulted and verbally abused him and his parents. The teacher told him that a child like him should be burnt alive. Even his parents should be banished from the society who has raised a child like him, when they went to confront her for her behaviour towards him. Pranab also had a traumatic experience in a Delhi hotel where he was approached by a waiter and they decided to meet. However, the waiter after entering his room in the night secretly opened the door and got a group of men and Pranab got sexually assaulted by all of them. He did not report this incident thinking he would not get the help, and it left a deep scare in him. Prankul our second participant, shared that he keeps facing harassment from the police in the hotspot areas. The police harassed him for money and alcohol which was a regular occurrence. He prefers to keep his gay identity a secret and therefore not involved with any organizations working with the gay community. Rajak experienced a violent outbreak in his village and was forced into a marriage by his family. These have left a bitter episode in his life and he does not want to go back to his native place. He has decided to live his life in Guwahati and never to go back to his native place. He also mentioned that he faces harassment from the police on a regular basis in the hotspot areas of gay men in Guwahati. Pinku one of the participants shared that who also work as apart time gay sex worker. Once his client took him to a hotel where there were three men. When Pinku refused to entertain all of them, he was abused physically and raped.

## Discussion

Same sex relationship is still a taboo in Assamese society and the narratives are the testimonies of it. During the study, it was found that the participants of the study were leading a discreet life of gay men soliciting other men in hotspot areas of Guwahati city except one participant who was engaged with his partner. All of them were self-identified gay men. However, their preferred sexuality was in the closet where they are not comfortable to talk about it openly. The visibility of their sexuality might bring out the unnecessary negative consequences. The participants of our study were professionals, daily wage earners and businessmen. In fact, one of them worked as a part time gay sex worker. Though there was fear of discrimination, violence and other possible harm in their daily lives the participants of our study preferred to identify themselves as gay men. They shared that their gay identity formation happened during their adolescent period. The study also revealed that the majority of them have experienced abuse and violence in their lives. The nature of violence was homophobic in nature followed by physical and sexual assault. The hatred and violence towards gay men is culturally legitimised, in fact few of them even complained of harassments they faced in the hand of the law enforcement authority. The police personnel harass them for money and at the same time insult them for their sexual orientation and gay identity.

Intersectionality of gender, geographical area/ethnicity, social norms and class are other dimensions which were observed among the participants of the study. Social class and geographical area/ ethnicity of the participants had an impact in their lives. Participants' self-definition of themselves at times did not recognize it but they did get affected and made a move to Guwahati city which can give them an obscurity to lead a life of their choice concerning their sexuality. Multiple identities of the participants of the study gave a distinctive individual experience and intersectionality acknowledges that.

It was found that their lack of a support system was one of the biggest challenges in their lives, which makes them even more vulnerable. There were exploitations happening to them due to their vulnerable position of being gay where social norms do not accept it in explicit terms. This nonacceptance of gay men marginalizes the participants of the study in many folds. Except for one participant of the study others did not display the stability in their relationships and lifestyle. Most of the participants of the study did not prefer to use condoms when they are in a steady relationship except during casual sex against sexually transmitted infections and HIV/AIDS though they were aware of it.

The study cannot be generalised due to the small sample size however, minority stress can be seen among the participants of the study. In fact, social stressors like discrimination, stigma or expectations of rejection, internalization of negative beliefs about one's sexual identity over the period can lead to Minority Stress situations. Same sex people frequently experience marginalization and stigmatization due to their relationships which eventually leads to a stressful situation. Minority Stress Theory (MST) was proposed by Meyer in 1995. He provided a theoretical basis for the effect of minority stress on the mental health of specific sexual minority groups, covering lesbian, gay and bisexual (LGB) people. In this context the participants of the study showed their vulnerable mental health situations at different points of time and none of the participants have worked on the trauma and abuse they have experienced so far. The trauma and sexual abuse have had left a mark on them which were never addressed though they were leading a preferred life of same sex relationships.

## Conclusion:

The study attempted to understand the lived experiences of the gay men in the city. During the study, it led us to comprehend the traumatic events and experiences of the participants. Though they are living their lives on their own terms, the participants of the study never ever addressed their traumatic experiences. The study reveals that there is a lack of support system for the gay men. Though there are few organizations none of the participants have received any help when it comes to their abuse and trauma. Most of the counselling and information provided by the organizations working for the gay community are on safe sex. The lack of sharing of their experiences from the perspectives of the participants shows that they themselves were weary of the expected help. In fact, two of the participants shared that they do not believe that these organizations can do anything as society is not progressive to accept them. There is a sense of isolation and learned acceptance of violence among the participants of the study. These needs to be addressed by the people working for the queer community so that there is a feeling of inclusiveness.

## Reference:


1. Aisner, A. J., Zappas, M., & Marks, A. (2020). Primary care for lesbian, gay, bisexual, transgender, and queer/questioning (LGBTQ) patients. The Journal for Nurse Practitioners, 16(4), 281-285.
2. Dadas, C. (2016). Messy methods: Queer methodological approaches to researching social media. Computers and Composition, 40, 60-72.
3. Meer, T., & Müller, A. (2017). "They treat us like we're not there": Queer bodies and the social production of healthcare spaces. Health & Place, 45, 92-98.
4. Stewart, S. J. F., Frost, D. M., & LeBlanc, A. J. (2019). Understanding how emerging same-sex couples make meaning of minority stress: A narrative approach. Journal of Family Psychology, 33(2), 183.

5. Tan, K. K., Treharne, G. J., Ellis, S. J., Schmidt, J. M., & Veale, J. F. (2020). Gender minority stress: A critical review. Journal of homosexuality, 67(10), 1471-1489.

6. Terra, T., Schafer, J. L., Pan, P. M., Costa, A. B., Caye, A., Gadelha, A., ... & Salum, G. A. (2022). Mental health conditions in Lesbian, Gay, Bisexual, Transgender, Queer and Asexual youth in Brazil: A call for action. Journal of affective disorders, 298, 190-193.

7. West-Livingston, L. N., Dittman, J. M., Park, J. A., & Pascarella, L. (2021). Sexual orientation, gender identity, and gender expression: From current state to solutions for the support of lesbian, gay, bisexual, transgender, and queer/questioning patients and colleagues. Journal of Vascular Surgery, 74(2), 64S-75S.

8. Worthen, M. G. (2022). Queer Identities in the 21st Century: Reclamation and Stigma. Current Opinion in Psychology, 101512.

# Non-binary Identity & Transgenders in India: Socio-Political Status of Hijras in Socio-Cultural Spaces of Assam

**Kaustav Padmapati**

## Abstract

Although 'eunuchs' or 'hijras' are part of the Indian society since ancient times and they occupy a paradoxical space in the binary gamut of male- female, they received legal and civil recognition only very recently in April 2014 with the Supreme Court of India declaring them as 'Third Gender'. Earlier they were forced to write male and female against their gender choices. Now they are recognized socially and economically as backward classes along with the category of Other Backward Classes (OBC). Although hijras are recognised as the "third gender" by the Indian state, they are still socially ostracized and discriminated against in almost all aspects of social and cultural life of Assam.

This paper proposes to examine the sociocultural exclusion and gender beliefs of the hijras and rethink their political identity in the Indian state with a special reference to Assam. It will try to locate the rights of the hijra, as a sexual minority in South Asia, within the context of mythology and socio-cultural spaces of India. The study will also focus on the vicious circle of brutality, challenges and interpersonal relationships between the members of the hijra community and other socio-cultural institutions of the society. While assessing the idea of two genders, and the introduction of the third gender category by the Indian nation-state, this paper will be an attempt to explore the possibilities of rethinking the identity of hijras in Assamese society particularly in the marginalized sections of the society beyond the three categories (male, female and third gender) of sex/gender model of the Indian state.

**Keywords:** *Identity, Sexuality, LGBTQA+, Hijras, Assam, Northeast*

## Introduction:

Trans identity or nature of gender is still contested or irrelevant in the socio-economic and political construct of the Indian state. Transgender as an identity is being rejected or labeled as unusual behaviour or mental sickness in mainstream Indian society. The traditional model of two genders/ sexes borrowed from the British Colonial system is imposed on all citizens including transgenders. This binary notion of gender restricts trans-men and trans-women, queer people and forces them to adhere to fixed notions of gender as male-female, further restricting their expressions of sexuality and sexual preferences. So, the Indian state constrains them to be an active partner of the socio-economic and political development of a society. The Indian state continuously discourages and forbids the marginalized sections of the society to live, practice, and express themselves in terms of their sexuality through its faulty policies, laws and anti-human rights rhetoric.

Although 'eunuchs' or 'hijras' are part of the Indian society since ancient times and they occupy a paradoxical space in the binary gamut of male-female, they received legal and civil recognition only very recently in April 2014 with the Supreme Court of India declaring them as 'Third Gender." Despite the legal recognition of "hijras," transgenders persons failed to occupy a socio-political space in Assam, a state in the northeast part of India. Transgender persons could be defined as those people who do not conform or fall under the binary notion of gender. But according to the historical records, transgender persons are omnipresent across different cultures even though a social stigma is assigned to them. Generally, transgender persons are referred to as those who deny traditional and socially accepted gender norms. They confront or challenge one of the most fundamental categories of human identity i.e. gender, including the fundamental ideas about the nature of social identity (Nagoshi et al. 2014). Their sexual identity is not similar to the gender that they were actually born. Referring to the binary norms of the gender, sexes were assigned to them during birth based on the physical attributes and appearances. Biologically transgender persons are generally not born with specific organs of either male or female. Sometimes they are born with biological organs of both the sexes or none of the sexes. The confusion of their sexual identity makes their life extremely complicated and challenging. Variety of terms is used to describe their unique gender identity like "non- binary" or "gender queer." As the transgender persons do not conform to the binary notion of gender identity, their experiences raise significant questions about the nature of socially defined identities (Nagoshi et. al, 2014).

Majority of gender experts agree that transgender is an umbrella term that refers to individuals whose gender presentation is different from ideals for the sex assigned to them at birth that it defies traditional notions of what it means to be male or female, and it encompasses identities such as transmen (or Female to Male), transwomen (or Male to Female), butch women, and crossdressers and is contrasted with being cisgender, or having a traditional gender presentation (Levitt, 2014). In common language, the interpretation of the term could be referred to those individuals or communities of individuals who transgress many social roles and responsibilities, around the notions of body, sex, gender and sexuality. The existences of Transgenders in the society are the testimony of their relations with the society and its social institution.

## Transgender and Indian History & Culture:

There are numerous references of diverse sexuality and genders in Indian history and culture. The Indian classical texts as well religious myths are full of examples of androgynous sexualities which are celebrated rather than shunned. With the advent of colonialism and its methods to contain sexuality under heterosexuality, gender also got contained as either male or female. The binary notion of gender turned out to be a norm since the colonial era and other genders are excluded from the socio-political and economic aspect of the society.

Unlike their colonial masters, the people of the Indian subcontinent have always been exposed to a "third" gender – the "non-male, non-female. Trans sexuality is seen as a transitional period either from woman to man or from man to woman in India. In ancient India, transgenders were also referred as "*tritiya prakriti*" or "*napunsaka*" or "not man," prakriti meaning nature, in Sanskrit means the third gender which would encompass any gender outside the dominant male and the female. The "*tritiya prakriti*," which was dominant and acceptable in the pre-colonial era were labelled as against the "order of nature," and rejected by the colonial masters. These terms were often loosely referred to a heterogenous group which included transsexuals, cross dressers, heterosexual transvestites, homosexuals who did not conform to the binary norms of the society.

A broad variety of transgender-related identities, characteristics and experiences could be found in India for examples: Hijras, Shiv Shaktis, Kinners, Kothis, Aravanis, Sakhi and eunuchs who have appeared in Indian literature and history and existed since 9th century BC (Mal, 2018). The most prominent and visible group among them are the hijras who are an integral part of Indian society. Hijras are mainly born biologically as a male but over a course of time refuse their "masculine identity." They prefer to classify either as "women" or in between men and women. They are mostly transsexual persons in Western context; however, in Indian context hijras form strong social bonding through forming their own community and identity. They face all sorts of discrimination in Indian society despite the Indian Constitution guarantees equality among the citizens. Transgender identity is complex, complicated and highly contested.

The term "hijra" includes multiple identities, which includes biological sex, gender identity and sexual activities, including historical references. Hijras are believed to belong to a third sex – neither male nor female. They are not male as they do not desire a sexual relation with women and not female as they cant give birth. "Hijras" are the only group of sexual minorities who received legal recognition in India as "Third Gender" in 2014. The term "third gender," refers to many transgender communities in South Asia. In simple terms, the hijras are the religious or cultural community of people who are neither men nor women but dress and act like women (Nanda, 1999). Prof Serena Nanda (1999) argued that the hijra role and identity appear to be adopted by people whose sexual impotence has a psychological rather than an organic source. So, in the Indian context, hijras include a broad variety of psychological, medical, and endocrine conditions and experiences.

In the 17th and 18th century, hijras wore both male and female clothing but after the 19th century, this portrayal changed to hijras only in women clothes and embracing attributes, customs and behavior. Also, the popular Hindu deity among Hijras is Lord Shiva in his *Ardhanarisvara* form who is half man/half woman. It represents the male form of Shiva united with his female/Shakti form. Hijras have a great affinity for Lord Shiva and are respected in Shiva temples." There are many temples dedicated to "*Ardhanarisvara*" in India. The state of Assam also has a "*Ardhanarisvara*," temple in Tarapur, Silchar. Both "Shiva" and "Shakti" are popular in Assamese Hindu society and folklore.

There are multiple examples in Hindu mythology that indicated hijras were inclusive in Indian society. These Hindu myths still empower the hijra community of India. Among the popular stories, which give power and strength to the community is the story about Lord Krishna's transformation to a woman to kill the demon "Araka," who was however a faithful demon. So, Krishna took the form of a beautiful woman, marries the demon and then kills him in a battle. After finally revealing the true self, Krishna announces "there will be many like me, neither man nor woman, and whatever words will come from the mouths of these people, whether good (blessings) or bad (curses), will come true "(Nanda, 1999). Even in the Hindu epic "Ramayana" there is also a reference of people who are neither man nor woman who waited 14 years for Lord Ram, the seventh reincarnation of Lord Vishnu. In addition to Hindu mythology, Sanskrit texts such as "*Natyasastra and Kamsutra*", there are instructions regarding "third gender."

In Hindu society, hijras are seen as sexually ambiguous figures. According to the popular Indian belief, hijras are "male bodied" people who undergo castration, as a sacrifice to Bachuchara Mata, an ancient Hindu goddess associated with gender liminality (Hossain

& Nanda, 2020). Their presence is desired or accepted during auspicious occasions like childbirth or marriage. However, the public attitude of the Hindu society towards hijras have been slow to change or is generally negative as they represent impotent men or eunuchs, so they are unwelcome. Their presence creates fear and anxiety in public places. The attitude is still hewing to colonial ideas about sexuality introduced by 19th century British colonial masters. The British Colonial rulers dramatically altered the prevailing cultural understanding of gender, attaching considerable stigma and discrimination to the hijra community that continues today. The British Colonial rulers dramatically altered the prevailing cultural understanding of gender, attaching considerable stigma and discrimination to the hijra community that continues today. According to Sapna Khatri (2017), currently hijras are treated as untouchables of 21st century India. Numerous social stigmas are associated with the entire community of hijras. Due to their gender non-conforming behaviour, hijras are subject to marginalization, economic deprivation, lack of opportunities for education, shelter, security and medical care. (Hossain & Nanda, 2020)

## Transgender in Assamese Society:

There is a huge gap between Hindu texts/mythologies and the state of contemporary socio- cultural Assamese society. Before colonial rule, hijras used to enjoy a better lifestyle working in wealthy homes. The Britishers challenged the broader meaning of gender in Indian society and created two contingent boxes of genders, male and female, and people were supposed to fall in these boxes. Those who does fall in the boxes or hang out at the edges or decide to be outside the boxes were labelled as an outcast. The Britishers introduced the draconian Indian Penal Code of 1860 which criminalized "carnal intercourse against the order of nature". They also dismissed the ambiguity in Sanskrit texts regarding sexualities and gender. India with its ambiguities was seen by the Britishers as in a complex state which needed civilization.

The traditional Assamese society was rural and patriarchal in nature, which was characterised by powerful sentiments of kinship locality, caste and community (Baruah 2020). Like any other patriarchal society in India, the birth of a girl child was undesirable for the parents in Assamese society. Traditional Assamese society did not see gender beyond the binary category. Surprisingly, there is not any record of transgender person in Assamese history. However, it does not mean that transgender persons were missing in Assamese society. Gender fluidity is visible in various socio- cultural spaces of Assam, including *Bihu* performances and *Raas Leela* performances. Practice of cross dressing is predominant in Assamese folk and Vaisavite culture. Cross dressing in "*Bhaona*[1]" and *Raas Leela*[2] performances have allowed many effeminate men and transgenders to survive in the rural spaces of Assam, as those societies are predominantly patriarchal. However, many of the male performers are not aware of their queer identity. The queer or transgender identity is shaped by histories of rejection, abjection and subjugation by the dominant patriarchal power structure. Being pushed to the periphery, the queers prefer fluid possibilities of gender and sexuality by debunking the false notion of compulsory heterosexuality (Hazarika 2022).

Although "hijra" identity in Assamese society is missing or closeted, Assamese language follows a three genders model. Assamese grammar has "*Kliba Linga*" or "third gender," in addition to masculine and feminine genders. "*Kliba Linga*" refers to inanimate objects which are neither masculine nor feminine. Commonly the term is also used to refer to Hijras and transgenders in Assamese society.

Sadly, the hijra community in Assam is the most backward and neglected community which is rejected and socially excluded from participation in any social activity. They are forced to live at the margin of Assamese society as the society fails to understand the psychological desires of a man who wants to live as a woman. Many scholars and experts

---

1 Bhaona is a performing art with religious messages mostly performed in rural Assam. It was introduced by Srimanta Shankar Deva, who pioneered the movement of Vaishnavism in Assam.

2 A festival celebrated during November in Assam, which was introduced by Sri Manta Shankar Deva.

put hijras in the same categories as crossdressers, transgendered individuals, eunuch transvestites, and male-to-female transsexuals, however, ignore the fact that the hijra are not simply a sexual orientation but also a well-defined social identity. The most crucial step to be "hijra" is to take the vow of "hijrahood," and become part of the hijra clan, which operates as a caste-based community with its own code of conduct, hierarchy, rituals, rules and regulations (Khatri 2017). Each clan has a "guru," or "leader," who is the head of the household and gharana. The guru performs all the duties as the head of the household and introduces the "hijra" way of life, which includes breaking all links with the heterosexual world. The hijra community is like a caste- based community based on hierarchy. After joining the "gharana" a novice sacrifices his male name and takes a female name in a symbolic rebirth and embraces female attire and manners. This symbolizes that hijras are almost women.

Unfortunately, the history of Assam is silent on other genders or third genders. Assamese society, as advanced as it claims to be, fails to acknowledge different gender identities and expressions. However, Hijras are referred to as "*Kinnar*" in Assamese society. According to a number of scholars from prominent institutions of Assam (Cotton University, Guwahati University, Tezpur University etc) hijras are new to Assamese society. Until early 2000, there wasn't much of culture of hijras or kinnars and their gharanas in Assam. Prior to this, many transgender persons from Assam, especially from the caste Hindu Assamese communities, went to Delhi, Odisha, Uttar Pradesh and Bihar. The period from 1980's to late 1990's in Assam was marked by militancy activities and disturbances so like migrants and students, who escaped the peak of militancy to study and work outside, many transgenders also left Assam looking for better job opportunities and wishing to find their identity. As things are slowly changing as sensitisation about the community is rolling in, many of them decided to return back to Assam.

Hijras are now frequently visible in the traffic signals, bus stops and popular public places in major cities and towns of Guwahati, Jorhat, Dibrugarh, Nogaon, Tezpur etc. "*Hijras*" are called by various names in Assamese like "Baido" and "Bhanti," (sisters) when regarded with respect, other popular terms are "*Maikimua*," and "*Napunsak*," when regarded with shame and mock. Undoubtedly, "hijras" are among the marginalized and backward communities in Assam politically as well as economically. Transgender persons in Assam face issues like abuse, bullying, rejection by family on a regular basis.

## Assamese Transgender's Political Identity Vs NRC:

In order to control illegal migration from nearby states, specially from Bangladesh, the National Register of Citizens (NRC) was implemented in Assam starting 2013-2014. The NRC is a register of all citizens whose main purpose is to verify all the legal citizens of India and identify all illegal immigrants for deportation. In Assam the process of updating of NRC started in the year 2013, when the Supreme Court of India passed an order for its update. On 31st August 2019, the final updated NRC for Assam was published with 3.1 crore names out of the population of 3.3 crore, leaving out 19 lakh applicants. Among the people left out and not included in the list were 20,000 transgender people of Assam. They were excluded as they failed to produce the required documents for NRC verification. The verification method of the NRC was uniform, based on a heteronormative understanding and documentary proof as evidenced by the NRC form. This process excluded the transgender persons and raised questions on their citizenship, trapping them in a complicated web of bureaucratic procedures and administrative barriers (Sharma, 2022).

Few trans women interviewed for this article in Guwahati did not submit an application to NRC Seva Kendra as they were not aware of the application process. None of them possessed any legacy documents like father or grandfather's name in the electoral etc. Also, sex assigned to them at birth certificates does not match with their gender. They have hardly any contact with their biological families, so getting access to lineage documents or proving linkages tracing a family tree was practically impossible. Political Scientist Chetna Sharma (2022) said that "document-based state practices fix an individual's identity, reflecting hegemonic ways of framing and labelling, and excluding those who do not comply with the set norms." All these efforts by the government create new forms of inequality in the state based on heteronormative structure.

There is a long history of resistance against the state-imposed regulations by marginalised communities. The transgender community from Assam was also no exception. On 1st September 2019, Assamese transgender activist and advocate Swati Bidhan Baruah, who is the first transgender judge in Assam, filed a last-minute prayer to issue guidelines for including transgender persons in the NRC within the ongoing writ petition at the Supreme Court of India. Although the gender identification section of the form had a choice for "others," all supporting documents needed to verify the existence of the individual prior to 1971 were based on the heteronormative framework. NRC was an exercise exclusively driven by patriarchal lineage, so transgenders in Assam were at the risk of exclusion and fear of alienation as most of their fathers and brothers have rejected them (Sitlohu 2018). When the state discourages and forbids the marginalized sections of the society to live, practice, and express themselves in terms of their sexuality through heteronormative policies and complicated documentation processes, a sense of isolation and exclusion emerge among them. The NRC in Assam created the sense of exclusion of transgender persons, proving how laws and their implementation are shaky.

## NALSA judgement and Political Identity of Transgender in Assam:

The political identity of "*hijras*" was always ambiguous in South Asia. The "hijra" category was added to the census in India only in 2011. The data about the real size of the transgender community is largely erroneous in India, particularly in Assam. There is hardly any accurate information, counting or scientific study about them in the state of Assam. Despite their seemingly invisible status in official records, members of the "hijra" community occupy a crucial space and are very much a part of public life. *Hijras* are visible in public spaces as it is a common sight in the cities of Assam like Guwahati, Jorhat, Tezpur, Dibrugarh, where hijras are begging or asking money in traffic signals, markets, public spaces. Among the Hindi-speaking communities of Assam, Hijras are invited to perform during any auspicious occasions, some of them also indulge in sex and prostitution. There are reports of abuse and violent clashes between hijras and civilians in Assam. Majority of these clashes happen due to the negative attitude of the society, which takes the form of withdrawal, disdain, anger, and violence. These negative and prejudicial responses are generally visible when members of the "hijra" community try to access their entitlements, claim public facilities or deal with homophobia.

The Indian state has been personally engaged with the lives of its citizens through rules and regulations on gender identity and sexuality through heteronormative policies. The hyper-masculine nature of the Indian state and its bureaucracy has been depriving its citizens especially the transgender and people of alternative sexualities to express their sexuality in the political and public domain. So the historic judgement about transgender persons' right to self-determine their gender was shocking.

On 15th April 2014, at the historic National Legal Services Authority (NALSA) vs Union of India case, the Supreme Court of India recognised "third gender"/ transgender persons and acknowledged "gender identity." The court also recognised that the third gender persons are entitled to enjoy fundamental rights under the Constitution of India. So, it directed all state governments to work on mechanisms to realise the rights of the "third gender" persons. In this historic judgement, the apex court upheld the right of all persons to self-identify their gender.

However, following the historical NALSA judgement there was hardly any visible significant systemic change in Assam for transgender community except the formation of All Assam Transgender Association (AATA) on 25th December 2015. According to the website of AATA, the association was formed with the help of the livelihood and establishment of transgender rights. However, ironically AATA was denied registration by the Government under the Societies Act as its formation may highly disturb the society and its peace. However, the founder Swati Vidhan Baruah went ahead and formed the association under Article 19 (C) of the Constitution of India, which comes under the fundamental right of freedom to form union and association in the territory of India. According to the AATA website, the association has the support of many legal counsels of High Courts and Supreme Court of India. Currently, AATA is providing free legal counselling to transgender and transsexual victims of domestic violence, sexual abuse and rape in Assam. In addition, AATA performs a number of activities to uplift the transgender persons' community of Assam.

## Socio- Political Status of "hijras":

Although hijras were granted legal voting rights in 1994, there are still ambiguities and challenges. In 2019, around 11,000 transgender voters were left out in the voting list of Assam. The amended electoral records issued on 1st January 2019 proved that the state hardly takes the concern of the transgender population seriously. On 26th November, the Government of India passed the Transgender Persons (Protection of Rights) Bill, 2019 on 26th November 2019 to get rid of various discrimination against the transgender community. The bill has turned into an act on 5th December 2019 with the assent of the President of India. Surprisingly, the Act did not make many members of the transgender persons' community happy. AATU also criticised the act as it was drafted and passed without consulting the members of the transgender community and assumptions were made based on outdated data and stereotypes. The constitutional validity of the Act was questioned by Swati Bidhan Baruah in a petition in December 2019, claiming many provisions of the Act "draconian" and "humiliating." Many provisions of the Act are not based on equality. According to Baruah, the most 'humiliating' provision as enshrined in the Act is that a transgender person cannot be self-identified as one (The Wire 2020). The Act has given the power to the District Magistrate who could only certify if someone is transgender or not. This provision itself is a clear violation of the 2014 NALSA judgement by the Supreme Court and right to self-identification. In the petition, Baruah mentioned that the Act violated fundamental rights of the transgender persons under Articles 14, 15, 16, 19 and 21 of the constitution. The Act is also silent regarding reservation, education, employment, and empowerment of the transgender community even treating the transgender persons' community as socially and educationally backward classes of citizens. In addition, the Act doesn't mention anything about civil rights like marriage rights, adoption rights, and property rights, etc.

## Assam Policy on Transgender 2020

The transgender population was hardly taken seriously in Assam. The transgender category was added for the first time in the 2011 census, which recorded 11,374 individuals who identify themselves as transgenders. However, a survey conducted by AATA states that the number of transgender populations has considerably increased to 20,000.

Following the Supreme Court's judgement regarding NALSA Vs Union of India case, the Assam Government through its Department of Social Welfare prepared a draft policy for uplifting the transgender population of Assam. It also aimed to understand the reasons responsible for the marginalization and vulnerable status of the community. Most importantly, it put emphasis on protecting the rights of the members of the transgender community. Through various steps, the policy wanted to create a discrimination free environment for the transgender community, recognition of their identity and it will be based on all gender's equality. The policy was approved by the Assam Government on 15$^{th}$ February 2020.

For the first time, the policy recognised the absence of trans friendly environments in educational institutions, workplaces and public places of Assam. Following the guideline of the policy, a six-member transgender welfare board was set up by the Assam government and members and grassroot activists from the state's transgender community were incorporated into the welfare board. Assam is the thirteenth state of the country to have such a welfare board, which aims at promoting awareness campaigns and sensitisation workshops to protect the rights of the transgender persons. The board will ensure non-discrimination of the members of the transgender community in public life as it possessed supervisory as well as quasi-judicial powers with power to issue summons. In addition, the board will make efforts for the upliftment of the community, by providing reservation in educational institutions, medical facilities, empowerment, and fight discrimination, among others.

The formation of the welfare board was a welcome change for the transgender community of Assam as the board aimed at implementing schemes meant for the transgender persons overall development. Unfortunately, the irregularities of the board started to emerge within a few years only. Responding to the irregularities, Swati Vidhan Baruah filed a public interest litigation (PIL) on two grounds. First, the Transgender Welfare Board has not been made fully operational till 19th January 2023 due to the absence of adequate infrastructural support, including an operational office. Secondly, the Assam Government has failed to take necessary steps for creating a State Level Transgender Cell as per the guideline of the policy. Petitioner Baruah mentioned that the failure on the part of the departmental authorities to initiate appropriate steps in such matters have resulted in violation of the statutory rights of the beneficiaries under the Transgender Person (Protection of Rights) Act, 2019 and the Rules framed thereunder. (All Assam Transgender ... vs The State of Assam and 7 Ors on 19 January, 2023)

The policies that transform transgender individuals into a legible, enumerated population by imposing a homogeneous category are not inclusive. There remains a consistent bias, rooted in patriarchal and heteronormative structures, the effect of which is to erase transgender individuals from the state's imagination. In Indian states, the recognition of transgender individuals has been limited to documents such as voter ID, Aadhar card, Passport etc. Almost a decade after the NALSA judgement, Indian law is ambiguous regarding the method for changing gender identity in papers. Due to the documentation verification process, transgender community can't move forward with the identity they have willingly chosen. (Sharma, 2022)

## Hijra Visibility in Public and Cultural Spaces of Assam:

The researcher interacted with a few members of the hijra community from various places of Assam. Surprisingly, the contradictory views came from different places. It seems hijras in the big cities are more vulnerable compared to the small towns of Assam. In the words of *Moina Baidew* (sister)[3], a mid-aged transgender member, from the Dolabari area of Tezpur town stated that she never faced discrimination in her neighbourhood for being different or effeminate. After schooling, Moina joined the hijra community in the Tezpur town area. She earns by performing and dancing on special occasions in the neighbourhood or begging on the street. Her village respects her and accepts her. However, she mentioned "as we are getting old, the government must give us pension to survive." So far, there is no financial scheme for the transgender persons of Assam.

Life is different for a hijra in a big city like Guwahati. The members of the community face harassment and abuse from the police. In addition, there are more challenges, the Hijra culture is still not popular or celebrated among the native indigenous Assamese, who neither fear their curses nor seek their blessings, stated by Saleha Khatun from Guwahati (Metro Area). Mostly the members of the "Gharana," perform song and dance for the Punjabi, Marwari and other Hindi-speaking families on special occasions in the city. As that earning is not enough, few members are engaged in sex work and prostitution.

Although Assam is lagging on a number of fronts in terms of recognition of LGBTQA + community, it became the first state in India to add a "transgender" option in the gender category in Assam Public Service Commission (APSC) examination form. As per the APSC data in 2020, a total of 42 transgender persons have applied for the combined competitive (preliminary) examination (CCE). Undoubtedly, this was a baby step for empowering the members of the transgender community. After a year, for the first time, the Government of Assam

[3] The author spoke with Moina Baidew over Phone.

officially invited around 25 inmates of a shelter home "*Tritiya Nivas*," for transgender people at the 74th Independence Day celebrations in Guwahati. The members of the community always desire for opportunities to actively participate in celebrations of state. Assam has over 26,000 transgender persons as claimed by a recent survey done by AATA. However, members of the community are facing a lot of hardship in earning their livelihoods due to absence of any adequate scheme for their economic upliftment. So many members of the community are engaged in begging and sex work as there was no programme for livelihood support to the transgender community. Reportedly, AATA wrote to all deputy commissioners of Assam seeking support for opening tea stalls to be run by the transgenders and Kamrup District deputy commissioner responded to the request. So, the first tea stall run by transgenders "Trans Tea Stall," was opened in the office premise of Kamrup District's deputy commissioner on 18th April 2022. The initiative was applauded by AATA as a modest beginning for empowering the transgender community.

In another welcome move, a tea stall run exclusively by transgender people was set up in collaboration with AATA at the Guwahati Railway Station on 11th March 2023. The tea stall was set up as a part of the Indian Government's comprehensive scheme for Transgenders named "Support for Marginalised Individuals for Livelihood and Enterprise." As transgenders are among the marginalized communities, the scheme included a sub-scheme for Comprehensive Rehabilitation for Welfare of Transgender Persons. Reportedly, the Guwahati Railway Station has become the first station of Indian Railway featuring a transgender run tea stall.

"Queer" visibility or references of "hijra" characters in Assamese popular culture is rare. Somehow "gharana" culture is alien to Assamese society and culture. According to David Lagachu (2021) "Regional films have always been a medium to showcase local culture to a wider audience and to include a queer character as a flavour of local Assamese social milieu is a both a pragmatic and radical step forward (galaxy)." Assamese filmmaker Prakash

Deka's debut film *"Jonaki Porua,"* took a radical step as it is, perhaps, the first Assamese feature film based on a transgender character in rural Assam. *"Jonaki Porua,"* tells the story of 'Jahnu' , a teenage boy's journey and fight to being Jahnavi, a transwoman, facing all the challenges in a village in Assam.

**Movie Poster:** Junaki Poruwa, Source : Max Player

In the movie, the protagonist feels trapped in a wrong body and struggles with gender dysphoria and ultimately embraces the preferred sexual identity facing all odds in a conservative society.

In the movie, "Jahnu's attraction towards feminine form of self-expression despite being assigned "male" at birth, lands him facing abuse and humiliation by the villagers. The movie was made with the intention to address homophobia and the stigma attached to being a transgender, enduring social discrimination and prejudice from the society (Lagachu, 2021). The main character in the movie was played by a young queer Assamese actor Benjamin Daimary. "Jonaki Poruwa," is produced by Milin Dutta, a well-known transman and an advocate of queer rights in Assam. Jonaki Porua, which highlighted the status of transgender community in India, won number of accolades, including National Awards, Assam State

Awards, Prag Cine Awards and shown in number of international film festivals like I AM Film Festival in London, Uganda Film Festival and FIPRESCI-India Grand Prix 2019 etc (Gani, 2020)

There are number of Assamese writers, artists and performers who supports LGBTQA+ community of Assam and advocates queer rights through their work. Prominent among them is popular Assamese singer Abhishruti Bezbaruah whose music video *"Ore Raati,"* released in May 2021 is inspired by the lived experiences of transgender person. The song is an attempt to focus on the internal struggle, acceptance of gender identity in society. In the song the singer urges society to embrace the transgender persons and empower them. Similarly, Assamese writer Tandrali Murchana released the first Assamese novel in 2022 based on full- fledged LGBTQ theme "Transgender," which is inspired by true events and addresses the issues of same sex love and sex change surgery. The book is definitely an attempt to foray into unfamiliar territory as Assamese literature does not have a space for queer literature.

In the last few years, Guwahati city also known as the gateway to northeast India saw a number of events to promote transgender rights and visibility. On 30th November 2022, the first ever beauty contest for transgender women was held in Guwahati to celebrate gender diversity and beauty. The beauty contest was organised by winner of Miss Trans Queen 2014 and fashion designer Ajan Akash Baruah to showcase more representation of trans women in Assam. Twenty transgender women from eight northeastern states of India participated in the contest showcasing the ethnic and tribal characters from each state. The transgender beauty contests are one of the platforms where the visibility of the transgender women is increased, and the beauty and the grace of the community members is displayed. These contests have the potential to turn into sites or platforms of transgender empowerment.

## The complexities of transgender identity in Assamese Society:

Majority of the Indian states do not protect transgender communities from discrimination based on their gender identity or gender expression. The members of the community face discrimination in nearly every aspect of their lives, which includes discrimination in employment, housing, health care, education, legal systems and even in their families. They face social stigma and prejudice and therefore have fewer opportunities as compared to other two genders. The majority of transgender people in India face social exclusion, which means inability of individuals to participate in economic, social, political and cultural activities at a normatively acceptable level. Discrimination of transgender community becomes more prominent over a period of time in the educational field. Sexual assaults and torture of a transgender student by fellow students are common in educational institutions in India. In addition to discrimination, transgender people suffer from multiple mental health issues due to abuse, non-acceptance of identity and feeling of isolation (Padmapati, 2021)

As already mentioned, Assamese society is predominantly patriarchal in its nature. The patriarchal nature of society supports and endorses masculinity as an accepted norm. Desire for a male child is an accepted feature of Indian society. So, most Assamese families do not tolerate it if their male child starts behaving in ways that are considered feminine or inappropriate to the expected gender behaviour. Transgender advance beyond the binary gender roles for which society did not have any space. For society it turned out to be a challenging task to reformulate any role and status for them. As a result, society reacts negatively or violently. Majority of people in the society mock or laugh at gender-variant people for being "different" and continue to discriminate. On the streets, transgender persons are harassed on a regular basis by the police. They face physical violence, verbal abuse, forced sex, money extortion and arrests on false allegations. Indian police hardly provide security and protection to the Hijra community, so they become the easy prey for demanding money and victim of sexual violence. So, the transgenders have no choice but to stay isolated from the regular society.

According to Milin Dutta[4], number of reasons could be identified why Assamese society is patriarchal and reactive against the transgender persons - lack of tolerance, dominating nature of patriarchal social norms and rituals, traditional approach of social institution, inadaptability of social beings for the acceptance any new behaviour, acceptance of heteronormativity and limited definition and functioning of gender and diversity. Society has a long way to go to be inclusive.

The transgender persons face exclusion due to the failure of the Assamese society to acknowledge them as a separate gendered identity beyond the male-female binary. Heteronormativity as being the accepted norm is dominant among all individuals and institutions, including families and the state. As an ideology, it tries to regulate the sexuality of all the members of the society irrespective of their class, caste, religion or gender in the effort to normalise the inequitable distribution of power, resources, spaces and other sources, resulting in a limited expression of human sexuality. Members of the *hijra* community lead a life of isolation due to the response they receive from the society at large, which includes withdrawal, disregard, violence, and rage from various actors. These reactions are generally visible when members of the community try to cross the barrier set by the heteronormative society, try to access the entitlement, public spaces, institutions etc.

Heteronormativity further deprives the "hijra," community from assimilating themselves in the society as humans with dignity, agency and security.

---

4 Based on the Thursday Discussion hosted by Anaajore, Panel Discussion with Kaustav Padmapati, Milin Dutta and Samhita Barooah, https://www.youtube.com/watch?v=XxHJMr9ESUk&t=2183s

## Conclusion:

Despite their apparently invisible status in NRC records, members of the transgender community occupy a significant place and are a crucial part of Assamese society. They clearly represent the "other," who remain outside the binary nature of the gender and therefore, one of the basic organising principles of social life. Will they remain marginalized? How does transgender identity be integrated within the Assamese identity?

Surprisingly, mainstream Assamese society still fails to accept those who venture beyond the male-female binary gender norm and therefore those who choose to live beyond this continuum become easy targets of discrimination, humiliation and shame. This further leads to a life without dignity for the hijras, whereby their deprivations are rooted in the non-recognition as a 'differently gendered' human being beyond the binary. It is obvious from the fact that mainstream society does not understand their culture, gender and sexuality, let alone their aspirations, hopes and dreams.

For any civilized society its public sphere must be inclusive and open to all sought of discussions. Trans-identity has been still considered a curse to a family and society. Due to the reluctance and ignorance of family and society; such identities have been excluded in public discourse. Attempts have to be made to discover potential queer or transgender identities in Assamese folk culture and rural spaces.

Dr Rehanna Kheshgi, Assistant Professor at St Olaf College, Minnesota, USA during her presentation of "Exploring Queer Potential in Assamese Bihu Performance," at an online session organised by Anajoree and hosted by the author (held in June 2022) pointed out potential discourse on queer possibility in folk culture performances of Assam, especially *Bihu* dance. Folk culture has often been used as a symbol to represent communities. One homogenised identity stands to represent the identity of the entire community. Similar ideas can be used for the *Bihu* festival and the Assamese community. Bihu, which is a harvest festival, is celebrated in Assam with great fun-fair and richness by all Assamese people irrespective of caste, creed, gender, religion, faith and belief. *Bihu* represents Assamese identity as the dance and festival has been used as a symbol for the creation of national unity and collective consciousness of the people of the region. It was an attempt to bring together ethnic groups which had been diverse at different points of history. Bihu is also the cultural arena where non-normativity is sanctioned. During her presentation, Dr Kheshgi raised the question – what does *Bihu* mean for queer and transgender persons? Can Bihu be used to imagine a more inclusive society?

With a message to stop gender-based discrimination and to create awareness about the transgender community, seeking their inclusion in festivals of Assam like *Bihu* a short video "*Ami Tritiyo*" (we, the third) was released by AATA in 2021. The main objective of the 2:24 minute video released on YouTube is to reject gender stereotypes and smash the patriarchal mindset that still exists in Assamese society. The video was made by AATA in collaboration with northeast Voluntary Association of Rural Development (NEVARD) as a part of a project by the social welfare department for mass sensitization on the issue of discrimination faced by the transgender community. Considered as the first public promotional ad film made in Assam with a hope for an inclusive society. As *hijras* are excluded from the sociocultural spaces and NRC documentation process in Assam, the references of methodology and popular text, Junaki Porua, Ami Tritiya, the novel "Transgender" open up potential discourse on transgender identity of Assam. As a progressive society, the Assamese society can progress towards a gender-inclusive society.

## References:


1. Agarwal, Palak (2021), Assam Transgender Community Releases 'Ami Tritiyo' Video Seeking Inclusion In Festivities, the logical Indian, available at https://thelogicalindian.com/lgbtq/assam-trangenders-video-festivities-25918
2. All Assam Transgender ... vs The State Of Assam And 7 Ors on 19 January, (2023), Kanoon, available at https://indiankanoon.org/doc/72660235/
3. ASSAM POLICY FOR TRANSGENDERS, (2020), Centre for Law and Policy Research, available at https://translaw.clpr.org.in/legislation/assam-policy-for-transgenders-2020/

4. Assam Becomes First State To Add 'Transgender' As Gender Option In Exam Application, (2020), https://www.india.com/news/india/assam-becomes-first-state-to-adds-transgender-as-gender-option-in-civil-service-examination-4190671/
5. Baruah, Archana, (2020), Position of Women in a Patriarchal Society with Reference to Assamese Society, *International Research Journal of Management Sociology & Humanity*, Vol 11 Issue 10, 302-304
6. Baruah, Pranjal, (2018), Assam NRC: Shunned by families, citizenship of many transgender individuals at stake as they fail to secure 'legacy data, Firstpost, available at https://www.firstpost.com/india/assam-nrc-shunned-by-families-citizenship-of-many-transgender-individuals-at-stake- as-they-fail-to-secure-legacy-data-5062251.html
7. Das, Gaurav, (2018), Interview | NRC Final Draft Is a Double Whammy for Assam's Transgender Community, the Wire, available at https://thewire.in/rights/nrc-assam-transgender-persons-supreme-court-nalsa
8. Das, Gaurav, (2020), Assam Govt Sets up Six-Member Transgender Welfare Board, the Wire, available at https://thewire.in/lgbtqia/assam-transgender-welfare-board
9. Das, Gaurav, (2020), Assam's First Transgender Judge Awaits Centre's Response to SC Plea Against 'Humiliating' Act, the Wire, available at https://thewire.in/lgbtqia/swati-bidhan-baruah-transgender-act
10. Das, Shreya, (2022), Empowering a community: Assam gets its first transgender-run tea stall in Kamrup, The Indian Express, available at https://indianexpress.com/article/trending/trending-in-india/assam-transgender-run-tea-stall-kamrup-7876131/
11. Deka, Rifa, (2022), I Decided To Pursue Law To Fight For Trans Rights: Assam's First Transgender Judge, outlookindia.com, available at https://www.outlookindia.com/national/i-decided-to-pursue-law-to-fight-for-trans- rights-swati-bidhan-baruah-assam-first-transgender-judge-news-205043
12. Devbrat, Kumar, (2023), Kudos To Indian Railways! In a First, Transgender Tea Stall Set Up At Guwahati Railway Station, H News, Available at https://www.indiatimes.com/news/india/transgender-tea-stall-set-up-at- guwahati-railway-station-595555.html
13. Dhar, Mugdha, (2021), Critical Analysis of Transgender Persons (Protection of Rights) Act, 2019, available at https://www.law-order.org/post/critical-analysis-of-transgender-persons-protection-of-rights-act-2019
14. Gani, Abdul (2020), Assamese film 'Fireflies' on LGBTQ theme, wins accolades, the News Mill, available at https://thenewsmill.com/2020/08/assamese-film-fireflies-on-lgbtq-theme-wins-accolades/
15. Gayatri, R (2010), *With respect to sex: Negotiating Hijras Identity in the south.* Chicago. University of Chicago press, E Book library
16. Guwahati Celebrates Gender Diversity With Transgender Beauty Pageant, (2022), outlook, available at https://www.outlookindia.com/national/

guwahati-celebrates-gender-diversity-with-transgender-beauty-pageant-photos-242287?photo-2

17. Hazarike, Nizara (2022) Transgressive Spatialities: Mapping Identity and Liminality in Contemporary Queer Narratives from Assam, *Rupkatha* Journal, Vol. 14, Issue 2, April-June, 2022. Pages: 1-11
18. Hossain, Adnan and Nanda S, (2020), Globalisation and Change among the Hijras of South Asia at Ryan, Michael 2020 (editor) Trans Rights in a Globalized Words – Rights, Identities and Politics, Routledge – Taylor and Francis, New York
19. Jain, Kalpana, (2022), For India's 'third sex,' acceptance is slowed by colonialism's legacy, religionnews.com, available at https://religionnews.com/2022/12/08/for-indias-third-sex-acceptance-mired-in-colonial-past/
20. Khatri, Sapna (2017), Hijras the 21[st] Century untouchables, *Washington University Global Law Review*, Vol 16 : 387 – 409.
21. Lagachu, David (2021), Queering Assamese Cinema: The Journey So Far, *Galaxy Magazine*, available at https://www.gaylaxymag.com/articles/art- culture/queering-assamese-cinema-the-journey-so-far/
22. Levit, Heidi M, (2014), Being Transgender: The Experience of Transgender Identity Development, *Journal of Homosexuality*, Volume 61, Issue 12
23. Mal, Sibsankar (2018), The Hijras of India: A Marginal Community with Paradox Sexual Identity, *Indian Journal of Social Psychiatry*, Volume 34, Issue 1
24. Meet Assamese singer Abhishruti Bezbaruah, who releases music video on real-life experiences of transgender people, (2021), NE Now News, available athttps://nenow.in/north-east-news/assam/meet-assamese-singer-abhishruti-bezbaruah-who-releases-music-video-on-real-life-experiences-of-transgender-people.html
25. Mohan, Ram, G, (2020), Halt Implementation of the Trans Act 2019: Activists, *the Wire*, available at https://thewire.in/lgbtqia/trans-act-2019-rules-feedback-activists
26. Nagoshi, Julie L, et al, (2014), *Gender and Sexual Theory – Transcending Feminist and Queer Theory*, Springer New York.
27. Nanda S. (1999), *Neither Man nor Woman: The Hijras of India*. Toronto: Wadsworth Publishing Company.
28. Nath, Anupam, (2022), Pageant celebrates transgender life in India, northwest weekly, available at https://nwasianweekly.com/2022/12/pageant-celebrates-transgender-life-in-india/
29. Nazir, Tasif, (2021), Freedom From Notions: Assam Invites Transgender Persons To Independence Day Function For First Time, the Ideological India, available at https://thelogicalindian.com/lgbtq/assam-invites-transgender-people-for-first-time-to-independence-day-function-30244
30. Padmapati, Kaustav, (2021), Gender Minority and the Indian State: The Political Identity of Transgender Community as Sexual Minority in India, Inclusive, Vol. II. Issue 19, PP 93-105

31. Prakash Deka's 'Jonaki Porua' all set to Conquer the Festival Circuit, (2020), *Kothasobi.com*, available at https://kothasobi.com/prakash-deka-jonaki-porua-film/
32. Sharma, Chetna, (2022), Hijras of Assam: undocumented 'citizens' in the National Register of Citizens, *Contemporary South Asia*, 30:2, 181-193
33. Sithlou, Makepeace, (2018), #NRCAssam: No state for transgender persons? Newslaundry, available at https://www.newslaundry.com/2018/08/15/nrc-citizens-list-assam-transgender

Unit 4

# Queer literature of Assam

# Queer Subjects in Selected Assamese Texts

**Anupom Kumar Hazarika**

## Abstract:

Literature brings social change and represents people who are discriminated against on the grounds of sexual identity, gender, and sexual orientation. For most Assamese readers, alternative sexualities are taboo subjects— they do not qualify as conversational topics. The presence of queer characters in Assamese literature is a relatively recent phenomenon, and Assamese queer literature has not been able to draw scholarly attention. Moushumi Kandali's short story "*Tritiyottor Golpo*" (2005) is an Assamese short story in which the protagonist is gay. Manikuntala Bhattacharya's *Mukti* published in 2006 is considered to be the first Assamese novel to deal with male homosexuality. In 2011, Dr Akashitora released her queer centric novel *Nisiddha* which comprises three stories narrated by a queer character. Adopting a queer theoretical framework, I seek to provide close readings of the afore-mentioned Assamese literary narratives that came out before 2018, the year when the Section 377 of the Indian Penal Code was declared null and void. In my analysis, I draw on Matt Houlbrook's discourse on the city to understand the correspondence between human sexuality and urban space and Judith Butler's notion of "livable life" to understand why the queer subjects in the narratives cannot embrace their queer selves. The essay ends with a positive note claiming that these three Assamese women writers subvert the Assamese literary imagination, and their material reality is the reason for the subversive nature of their queer narratives.

**Keywords:** *Assamese, gender, narrative, queer, sexuality, subjectivity*

## Introduction:

In 2012, I heard about an Assamese fiction in which homosexuality was represented.[1] I got the book as a gift from one of my friends who told me that the book centered around male homosexuality. Not only had I learned about the fair youth immortalized by William Shakespeare in his sonnets, I had also watched a few queer movies, especially Hollywood movies. Before I went through the book, I presumed that the book would challenge stereotypes about gay men. Unfortunately, I could not finish the book.[2] I should not have jumped to the conclusion that the book would be a beacon of hope for the Assamese reader. As I asked Aruni Kashyap[3], a bilingual writer who writes in Assamese and English, about his take on the book, he expressed dissatisfaction at the way male homosexual behaviour was represented in that Assamese fiction. Just because it is a gay novel does not mean that it humanizes gay men.[4]

Objectives and Theoretical Framework:

Having narrated my unpleasant experience, I now move on to discuss the objectives of this essay and explain the significant theoretical concepts without which a queer theoretical reading is hardly ever possible. This essay is about neither how you should write a good Assamese queer poem/ novel/short story/ nor the tools which can help you count an Assamese text as a great example of Assamese queer literature. Additionally, I do not seek to chart any genealogies of Assamese queer literature in this essay. In the beginning, I would like to explain the meaning of the phrase "Assamese queer literature" since this multi-word phrase is a neologism which one cannot expect to come across it in any

---

1 The book became the first Assamese gay novel.

2 The novel was Mukti (2006) by Manikuntala Bhattacharya.

3 Aruni Kashyap in his book His Father's Disease and Other Stories creates Assamese queer characters. In fact, the title of his short story collection is named after the queer story "His Father Disease" in which the wife considers homosexuality as a disease.

4 Aruni Kashyap in one of his interviews says that Mamoni Roiswam Goswami was the first Assamese writer who treated the queer subject sensitively. For more information, see Pisharoty (2020).

dictionaries. "Assamese queer literature" encompasses writings by Assamese writers who write about queer people and their lives, and the target audience for Assamese queer literature are people who can understand the Assamese language. This essay sets out with the aim of providing close readings of three Assamese narratives situating them in the socio-cultural context responsible for the production and reception of the narratives. Drawing on a queer theoretical framework, the essay seeks to examine how queer desires/intimacies are represented in the three texts and how these regional narratives redefine the conventional notion of "family" and reconceptualize human sexuality. Besides, I, in my analysis, draw on a few key thinkers' discourses on "the city" to understand the nexus between sexuality and urban space. The body of literary texts I analyze comprises one Assamese short story— "Tritiyottor Golpo" by Moushumi Kandali— and two Assamese novels— *Mukti* by Manikuntala Bhattacharya, and *Nisshidha* by Dr Akashitora. Before I discuss the afore-mentioned literary texts, I like to explicate these key terms— homosexuality, sex, gender, and sexuality— which were first theorized in the West because I rely heavily on them while I closely read the chosen queer narratives. The poststructuralist turn in Western philosophy takes a skeptical approach towards language and demystifies the power dynamics in binary relationships—colonizer/colonized, day/night, human/ nonhuman, heterosexual/ homosexual, men/women, and so on.

Michel Foucault (1998), a poststructuralist philosopher, in his book *The History of Sexuality* discusses how human sexuality was brought under the legal purview and claims that medical discourse identified the homosexual as a new category of species— "The nineteenth-century homosexual became a personage, a past, a case history and a childhood, in addition to being a type of life, a life form, and a morphology, with an indiscreet anatomy and a possibly a mysterious physiology" (p. 43). It is also echoed by Donald E Hall (2003) who says "homosexual" and "heterosexual" too are recent identifiers, dating from late nineteenth-century medical terminology. They are not at all accurate as terms for labelling identities from previous centuries, though they are useful for describing specific activities between members of the same sex or different sexes"

(p. 25). This demarcation led to the emergence of sexuality as an identity marker. Sexual identity, gender, and sexuality are key terms in queer studies. Though sex and gender are used interchangeably by people, they have different meanings in the context of feminism and queer studies. As Marlene Mackie (1987) explains: "Sex" refers to the physiology and "gender" to the socio-cultural elaborations upon physiology. To go a step further, sex roles (behaviors stemming from biological sexual differences) may be distinguished from gender roles (socially created behaviors differentially assigned to men and women)" (p. 3). In a similar vein, Barry Rutland (1997) says, "gender is a secondary formation grounded in biological reproductive sex but distinct from it, as a building is distinct from and heterogeneous to the land on which it stands" (p. 1). Mackie and Rutland reiterate Judith Butler as their claims about sex and gender are congruent with hers, yet Butler extends her argument further because she explains how the sexed body overlaps with its gender identity. Alluding to the nature/ culture binary, Butler (1993) says that sex, like nature, is "a site or surface of inscription" and gender, as a cultural construct, is "imposed upon the surface of matter, understood either as the body or its given sex" (p. 2). Gender, in the words of Butler, is "the social significance that sex assumes within a given culture" (Butler, 1993, p. 5). My usage of the terms "sex" and "gender" is in accordance with theirs, and I draw upon the definition of "sexuality" suggested by Kimberley Tauches. Tauches (2012) writes, "sexuality can be an identity or an act" (p. 173). To put it simply, sexuality, as an identity, depends on the object of desire that an individual craves for, and it, as an act, is based on the sexual acts which an individual performs to either get pleasure or reproduce. In the section that follows, I discuss the lack of the academic literature on regional queer literature and assert the significance of academic inquiry.

The dearth of scholarly articles/essays on regional queer literature[5] on the Internet evinces the negligence of literary scholars— either

[5] Regional literature means literature produced in regional languages of India.

Indian academicians believe that regional writers are oblivious of/have not written about queer issues, or their first choice is not regional queer literature because an analysis on regional queer literature may not reach a wide audience. In fact, Brinda Bose's essay in *The Cambridge Companion to Gay and Lesbian Literature* focuses on Indian English queer literature. As far as discussions on Indian queer writings are concerned, there are many academic essays/reviews/discussions on queer literary texts written in English. No doubt, Ruth Vanita's meticulous approach to Indian queer writings is reflected in her book *Queering India: Same-Sex Love and Eroticism in Indian Culture and Society* in which she demonstrates the implicit queer subtexts in early Indian literature. Yet, the book does not cover all regional writings. Is there not any queer subtext in the regional texts which Vanita excludes? I would like to answer it in the affirmative— one can read Maheswar Neog's *Guru- carita-katha*[6] through a queer critical lens. If one attempts to create a list of queer literary writings from the Indian subcontinent, one must be very careful as there is a colonial hangover at work, which involves overlooking literature written in regional languages of India. Alluding to the self/other binary, one can argue that the north-eastern part of India qualifies as "the other" and employ the appendix as a metaphor to explain the treatment received by this region which does not garner much attention from mainland India. Literature in English from this region was not counted as proper examples of Indian English Literature. This is evident in books such as *A History of Indian English Literature* by M.K Naik and *A Concise History of Indian Literature in English* by Arvind Krishna Mehrotra in which one cannot find any entries on anglophone North-east literature. Assamese queer literature is subject to double exclusion— Firstly, Assamese is not the language of the elite, secondly queer sexuality is on the periphery of human sexuality. This essay is written in support of Peter Jackson (2000) who advocates studying the existence of queer lives in non-western countries:

[6] It is a biographical account of Vaishnava saints of Assam.

> We lack studies of the changes in economics, social organization and political systems which have created the spaces for the emergences of Asian gay and lesbian scenes. Current histories, ethnographies, and sociologies of gay and lesbian identities are overwhelmingly from the West, and we need studies of gay Bangkok, gay Seoul, gay Mumbai, gay Taipei and other major Asian cities that are as detailed and as comparative as those we have of gay Sydney, gay New York, gay London and gay Amsterdam. (p. 1-2)

## Moushumi Kandali's "Tritiyottor Golpo" (2005)

Moushumi Kandali is a literary writer, art critic and translator. Kandali, who has both fiction and non-fiction to her credit, began her literary career with her short story "*Junakot Dhekiabur*" which she wrote when she was pursuing her graduation at Cotton College in Guwahati. Till now, she has published three short-story collections in Assamese—*Lambada Nachor Seshat* (1998), *Tritiyottor Golpo* (2007) and *Mockdrill* (2010). Kandali is recognized as a powerful women writer who has shaped the genre of Assamese short story. Her short stories are complex, full of symbols and ambiguities. Her foray into the human psyche and her attempt to dramatize the inner thoughts of her characters set her apart from other Assamese short-story writers. Her second book is named after the eponymous story "*Tritiyottor Golpo*". Included in the second collection, "*Tritiyottor Golpo*" first appeared in the Assamese weekly, *Sadin*, in 2005. The plot tells the story of a divorced gay man, a lecturer by profession. Kandali adopts a first-person narrator, unnamed and ungendered, chronicling the doings of the professor. The chief protagonist is represented as an unconventional man who does not fit into the straightjacket of masculinity. Before his divorce, he is in a relationship with a man named Sanjay who is also his live-in partner. Both of them find it difficult to carry on their secret relationship and end up marrying women. After his breakup, the professor marries a woman named Chitra. Regrettably, they cannot find a way to work out their marital issues, and she leaves him one day without informing him. He organizes dance recitals at his house and invites his friend Maitreyi and the narrator. Upon seeing Maitreyi pregnant, he tells her that he wants to conceive too. The professor, at last, finds the purpose of his life. At the end of the story, he rescues a girl child from a religious conflict and decides to raise her as his own kid.

To understand how Kandali characterizes her protagonist, it is significant to consider both his gender identity and his preferred sexual orientation. The professor is a subversive person in terms of the gender he likes to identify himself with. The narrator informs that the man likes to wear silver bangles and keeps long hair. Whatever he puts on functions as a sign. As he sits for job interviews, the transgressive aspect of his gender identity unsettles the employers ending up overlooking his academic contributions. Moreover, the general public send disapproval letters to him stating that he may face stiff penalties for being a threat to Indian culture. Men behaving like women or trying to transgress gender norms are seen as a threat to the social-cultural foundation of gender roles. Kandali protagonist is radical as he does not pay any heed to people's speculations about his way of life. As he is a person of artistic inclination, he organizes dance recitals at his house. Besides his friends, he invites singers belonging to the Harijan community who live close to his place. The narrator says, "It was in the Maitreyi's soulful rendering of the *Deshakshi raga* that night, that I saw him transforming into an *Abhisarika nayika* waiting for the loved one" (Kandali, 2021, p.286). The professor's abode in the city functions as a liberating space where the division between the upper-caste and the lower-caste are dissolved and the gender binary is subverted. He is an ardent admirer of Akka Mahadevi, a female poet who lived in the twelfth century. His fascination for this poet who denounced conventions and accepted a spiritual outlook towards life at an early age reaffirms the protagonist's worldview. Kandali (2021) narrates,

> Third! Third again! Third-third-third-why was he obsessed with the third number— the number three? He preferred a hotel room with the number 3. He was fond of cubism. His favourite story was 'The Third Bank of the River,' Shiva's third eye. The three-dimensional representation— the reality

> of the third world— politics, economics, sociology. He liked all the legends of the third hell. (p. 285)

For him, the signifier "third" means something that is beyond the logic of binary opposites. Kandali's (2021) story deconstructs the gendered aspect of motherhood— "...we think motherhood is only for women...one does not require a womb to be a mother—all one needs is a womb of sensitivity and emotion..." (289). Rescuing a girl from a conflict zone, the professor decides to raise her, who is named after his favourite poet, Mahadevi. The intersection of place and human sexuality has drawn the attention of many scholars such as Lawrence Knopp, George Chauncey, Pat Califa, Richard Sennett and Matt Houlbrook. Here, I would like to draw on Matt Houlbrook (2005) observations on the productive force generated by the city. Citing the example of a boy named Cyril who came to London in 1932, he says London is "a productive space that generates and stabilizes a new form of selfhood and a new way of life" (p. 3). Kandali chooses an urban space as the setting of her story. Her first-person narrator informs the reader that the protagonist used to share his house with his live-in partner Sanjay. Both the professor and Sanjay can embrace their queer selves as the city, as argued by Houlbrook, generates new forms of selfhood. But they have to end their relationship because of Sanjay's familial obligations. Sanjay's father begs him for his son's disentanglement from the professor's influence. The sympathetic professor cannot but discontinue their relationship. As the first-person narrator does not provide much information about Sanjay, the reader cannot be sure about Sanjay's sexuality— he may be either gay or bisexual. As far as queer intimacy is concerned, it is significant to pay attention to the way the narrator describes it. The first-person narrator says, "The cumin-cardamom scented kitchen air: towels, vests, and bedsheets on the clothesline flapping in the breeze eagerly to be soiled again" (Kandali, 2021, p. 287). Kandali's imagery appeals to the reader's senses— the sight of the towels and their vests. The usage of the verb "soiled" carries a sexual connotation. The narrator heavily sexualizes the intimacy between the two men.

An important aspect of Kandali's short story is that it is marked by postmodern elements. Her unnamed narrator and her central protagonist have one thing in common— their favourite story is Joao Guimaraes Rosa's 'The Third Bank of the River'. Rosa's story, originally written in Brazil, is a story about a man who tries to get rid of familial responsibilities and embarks on an unusual voyage. The protagonist of Kandali's story is addressed as "the living story" or he is, according to the narrator, a living manifestation of Rosa's story. Like Rosa's central character, he does not let social codes delimit his life. The professor's body functions as a metaphor for a postmodern literary text that defies the logic of fixity.

## Manikuntala Bhattacharya's *Mukti* (2006)

Manikuntala Bhattacharya is a prolific Assamese writer who has won many literary accolades. Her oeuvre includes four poetry books, six short story collections, twenty-two novels and four books of non-fiction. *Mukti*, her third novel, came out in 2006 and has also been translated into Hindi. Told from a third-person point of view, *Mukti* narrates the story of Smriti Bhattacharya (the author's surrogate) who is a writer by profession. Smriti, married, is a city dweller. She is introduced to Roshan Seth who lost his brother to AIDS. After the death of his brother, Seth is associated with an NGO working for the disadvantaged. Together with Seth, Smriti visits the slum areas in Guwahati to learn about the people inhabiting those spaces. Bhattacharya's novel depicts people existing on the margins of society, economically poor people, prostitutes, and slum-dwellers. Seth introduces Smriti to Basanti who runs a prostitution ring. Smriti gets to know that Basanti's elder son lives with Seth. This aspect of Seth's character, the humanitarian service he provides to people, sets him apart from Smriti and other characters. One day, as she visits Seth's house, she discovers that Shankar has murdered Seth. Smriti finds it difficult to comprehend how Shankar could even think of killing the person who is a role model for other people. Later, she learns from Shankar's mother that Seth used to sexually abuse Shankar. At the end, Smriti decides to educate Shankar, thereby fulfilling her void of not having any children.

For her story, Bhattacharya chooses a third person limited narrator who from the beginning to the end is centered on the central protagonist, Smriti. At the end of the novel, the narrator reveals why Shankar has murdered Roshan Seth. As Smriti catches onto the fact that Seth nagged the boy to have sex, she realizes that Roshan Seth is perhaps a homosexual man. The third-person limited narrator does not let the reader have any access to Seth's thoughts. The reader learns about Seth's sexuality from Smriti whose perspective is foregrounded by the writer. Seth's non- normative desires are interpreted by Bhattacharya's cis-gender protagonist whose doubts about Seth are reaffirmed by the tragic incident. In contrast to Smriti who learns how not to live in the past, Seth remains a flat character in the narrative. He neither develops throughout the novel nor succeeds in drawing sympathy from the reader. In this Assamese novel, homosexuality is represented as an aberration, and the reader cannot help but see a misrepresentation of male homosexual behaviour. The moral of *Mukti* is that either the repression of homosexual desires converts men into pedophiles or all homosexual unmarried men are sexual predators.

Bhattacharya's protagonist is biased against the have-nots. Despite being a writer, Smriti cannot develop empathy for everyone. As Smriti is an upper-caste woman who has never been unlucky except for the death of her newborn child, she fails to acknowledge the fact that people who are from the lower strata of society are exploited economically by the haves. Her judgements are clouded by preconceived ideas that make her judge people based on their social classes and professions. This is evident in her attitude towards Basanti, Shankar's mother. Smriti does not put any effort to find out why Shankar murdered Seth. When Basanti arrives at her house, Smriti treats her with indifference. Smriti believes that it is pointless to do something in favour of the disadvantaged. Likewise, Rupak, Smriti's husband, tells her not to rely on Basanti's words. He warns her that they are manipulative and untrustworthy. Bhattacharya ends her novel with Smriti consulting a lawyer who will fight Shankar's case in the court. She tells Basanti that she will educate Sankar and asks her to release the children kept for prostitution. The ending of the novel reinforces Smriti's weltanschauung. Smriti stands out as a morally good cis-gender upper -caste woman whose perspective may affect the queer reader who cannot find his/her lived experience representing authentically in the text. Bhattacharya's text reaffirms compulsory heterosexuality and the natural correlation between sex, gender and sexuality, thereby erasing the lived experience of being gay and alienating the inclusive reader from experiencing aesthetic pleasure. As Judith Butler (2009) argues,

> The epistemological capacity to apprehend a life is partially dependent on that life being produced according to norms that qualify it as a life or, indeed a part of life. In this way the normative production of ontology thus produces the epistemological problem of apprehending a life, and this in turn gives rise to the ethical problem of what it is to acknowledge or, indeed, to guard against injury and violence. (p. 3)

## Dr Akashitora's *Nishiddha* (2011)

Dr Akashitora is an Assamese writer whose stories center on urban life. Put out in 2011, *Nishiddha* comprising three stories is a fiction narrated by Soumar Kakoti who happens to be a psychologist. The first story, which is the story of an artist, titled "*Ji Kotha Nohol Kuwa*" is written in the epistolary mode, while the second "*Kot Je Asila...*" and the third "*Nishiddha*" follow a conventional plot structure. The novel begins with forty-something Soumir Kakoti in his chamber. Atul Barua, a journalist visits him with the express purpose of interviewing him. Informing him that a jawan shot himself dead because his lover had decided to marry a woman, Barua tells him that he wants Kakoti's opinions on male homosexual relationships. Kakoti says to him that he will tell him three stories. These three stories, as Kakoti says, are based on people he has come across. "Ji Kotha Nohol Kuwa", the first story, is about a divorced artist named Abhimanyu Chaliha who is a forty-year-old artist. He likes to put on women's clothing and identifies himself as a woman. After his divorce, he feels lonely and begins to suffer from insomnia. When Suruj Lochan Barua, an art critic, reviews his art, Chaliha calls him and thanks him for appreciating his work. Art brings the two of them together. Chaliha immediately falls in love with Suruj who is married to Rumi and has two kids. He does not think twice about the ramifications of falling for someone who has a lot of familial responsibilities. Suruj is presented as a confused individual who does not reveal to the reader about his sexuality. The reader learns from the first-person narrator, Abhimanyu, that Suruj is perhaps a bisexual man. Suruj himself never says who he is attracted to most. In the end, Suruj turns out to be a hypocrite man who involves himself in sexual liaisons and treats Abhimanyu like a bait so that he can climb up the social ladder. He prefers physical intimacy to love and cannot muster up courage to tell his wife about his relationship with Abhimanyu. The second story in the novel revolves around two women— one is married, another single. Jharna Barua, an engineer by profession, bumps into Rubi Bora at a party organized for the employees of ONGC, Duliajan. Rubi is married to Rupak and is the mother of two children. Rubi finds the glitz and glamour of any party repulsive. She attends the parties because of her husband who misbehaves with her and does not let her live her life according to her own terms. Rubi is frustrated with her husband who calls her "cold coffee" and slangs her. After she meets Jharna, Rubi's life takes a drastic turn. Jharna encourages her to revive her lost interest, in singing. They go out and share each other's joys and sorrows. They also secretly get married in a temple. As Rupak learns about their secret relationship, he beats Rubi badly. Rubi decides to end her life by cutting her wrist with a blade. This story climaxes with the women moving on from Assam to Australia. The third story is about two cousin brothers— Nibir and Nirob— who are caught while making love to each other. Hailing from a small village named Juktoli, they run away from their homes before they are caught by the villagers who will punish them for their immoral behavior. Nibir joins a car garage, while Nirob is hired by the owner of a beauty parlor. The latter becomes a famous make-up artist in Guwahati. A co-worker takes the former to a prostitute's house. Arrested during a police raid, Nibir spends two years in jail. He indulges himself in sexual liaisons with random people. Nirob loses one of his friends who is blackmailed by a group of people. They leak her MMS forcing her to commit suicide. Frustrated, Nirob visits Soumir Kakoti's chamber to regain his masculinity. Eventually, Nibir and Nirob decide to go back to their village as the city has disillusioned them.

Abhimanyu's story and Rubi's story chart the lives of the haves. The four characters— *Abhimanyu, Suruj, Jharna, and Rubi*— are educated and privileged with regard to the social class they belong to and their caste affiliations. *Jharna* is influenced by transnational queer identities, hence she can dream of an alternate future. She tells *Rubi* about mainstream western queer couples who she met and assures her that she too can dream of an alternate life. Likewise, *Abhimanyu* settles for breaking off his affair with *Suruj* because he does not have any other entanglements. On the contrary, *Nirob* and *Nibir* have fewer options in the city. Either they can remain anonymous forever in the city, or they must return to their loved ones in the village. The three stories touch on the hypocritical nature of the upper class. *Abhimanyu's* lover *Suruj* turns out to be a cheater who plays with *Abhimanyu's* emotions and sleeps with multiple women. *Rubi's* husband is a sadist person who never tries to act compassionately with *Rubi*. The deceptive nature of the haves is portrayed in the way they behave at informal gatherings. Any informal gathering creates a highly charged atmosphere. The parties *Rubi* goes to happen to be male dominated spaces where men, who are heavily drunk, do not follow social codes and objectify the female body. The female body becomes a site where they try to dramatize their repressed sexual urges. *Rubi* cannot raise her voice against physical harassment as that will lead to unexpected circumstances. This shows how the exploitation of her body is naturalized in public spaces and implies how indecency becomes an acceptable form of behavior in the parties organized by the upper class. The second narrative is the only story with two radical characters— *Jharna,* who does not comply with gender norms, has been a subversive person since her childhood, and the reader sees *Rubi*'s transitioning from a submissive woman to a vocal person. In the third story, the author attributes two different personalities to the two central characters. Right from the start, *Nibir* uses his cunning and clever tricks to not only fool people but also to survive. Disguising himself as a deaf and dumb person, *Nibir* cheats the bus conductor while they are travelling to Guwahati on a bus. He is arrested during a police raid, and later he contracts the HIV virus. *Nirob* has a moral outlook towards life. He, in fact, tells *Nibir* that he must pay for the sins he committed. *Nirob* justifies his state of affairs by comparing it with the other's predicament. *Nirob* does not express any feelings towards any girl, nor is it revealed that he is either heterosexual or bisexual. He is influenced by Soumir Kakoti who tells him that transvestism determines people's sexuality. Nirob thinks that his friends who like to cross-dress will be cured one day. Nirob seeks to unlearn his feminine behaviour and decides to marry a girl. It is a reaffirmation of the notion of gender essentialism. The ending of the third story is problematic because it proves the author as illogical in terms of her approach towards gender and sexuality—the third story represents homosexuality as curable. The narrator of the three stories, Soumir Kakoti, tells the journalist at last that he is gay. Besides narrating the three stories, Kakoti remains a flat character who does not play any significant role throughout the novel.

## Conclusion

Pain, together with torture, mark queer narratives, and "*Tritiyottor Golpo*" and *Nisiddha* are no exception. Kandali's story is the most authentic attempt at upholding the lived experience of being queer — her character not only challenges the gender binary but also does not hesitate to embrace his queer self. Also, her protagonist does not validate any essentialist notions concerning parenthood and sexuality. Likewise, the characters—Abhimanyu, Jharna, and Nirob—in *Nisiddha* succeed in subverting the gender binary, and the two lesbian characters, Jharna and Rubi, not only embrace their queer selves but also get out of experiencing forced heterosexual behaviour. *Mukti* reinforces queer stereotypes and likens queer sexuality to a form of anomaly, and, as a result, it fails to contribute much to challenging prejudice against the homosexual man. Bhattacharya's characterization proves her as a biased cisgender writer who cannot authentically portray her gay character's lived experience. Unlike Western queer narratives in which "coming out of the closet" is represented as an imperative to the construction of queer subjectivity, the three Assamese queer narratives do not touch on the trope. The fate of the queer characters in their narratives is largely determined by the imagined socio-cultural context. The historical context is important to demystify why the characters hesitate to embrace their queer selves, and why queer "livable lives' (Butler, 2009, p. 21) for them remain a distant dream. These texts came out before 2018, and the stories share a similar setting— pre-2018 Assam. The three authors could not represent a queer livable life as it could not be produced according to the norms of Assamese society. The lack of scholarly papers and reviews on these texts reveals that Assamese queer literature is not a growing area of research. As far as fictional writings on the Assamese queer subject are concerned, there are other Assamese women writers representing queer lives in their writings. A few notable examples include Anuradha Sharma Pujari, Maini Mahanta, Rudrani Sharma and Juri Baruah. Most Assamese queer narratives including the ones which I discuss here are by women, which establishes Assamese women authors as more subversive than their male counterparts. Women authors' material reality is the reason for the proliferation of imaginary Assamese queer characters. Their subjugation allows them to question their ontological identity, and queer lived experiences which are out of the ordinary reflect their feminist articulations. Queer sexuality was a new terrain for the chosen writers; however, the cisgender women authors' attempts are laudable as writing about the queer subject signals a new beginning in Assamese literature. Their writings have made the Assamese queer subject visible, thereby challenging the reader's normative understanding of human sexuality and disturbing the correlation between sexual identity and sexuality.

## References:


1. Bhattacharya, Manikuntala. (2006). *Mukti*. Purbanchal Prakash.
2. Bose, Brinda. (2014). Notes on Queer politics in South Asia and Its Diaspora. In E.L. Mccallum and Mikko uhkanen (Eds.), *The Cambridge History of Gay and Lesbian Literature* (pp. 498-511). Cambridge University Press.
3. Butler, Judith. (1993). *Bodies That Matter*. Routledge.
4. Butler, Judith. (2009). *Frames of War: When is Life Grievable?*. Verso.
5. Dr.Akashitara. (2011). *Nishiddha*. Banlata.

6. Foucault, Michel. (1998). *The History of Sexuality*. Penguin.
7. Hall, Donald E. (2003). *Queer Theories*. Palgrave Macmillan.
8. Houlbrook. Matt. (2005). *Queer London: Perils and Pleasure in Sexual Metropolis*, 1918-1957. The University of Chicago Press.
9. Jackson, Peter. (2000). *Pre-Gay, Post-Queer: Thai perspectives on Proliferating Gender/Sex Diversity in Asia*. In Peter A. Jackson and Gerard Sullivan (Eds.). Harrington Park Press.
10. Kandali, Moushumi. (2021). A Tale of Thirdness. In Mitra Phukan (Ed), *The Greatest Assamese Stories Ever Told* (pp. 283-290). Aleph.
11. Mackie, Marlene. (1987). *Constructing Men and Women: Gender Socialization*. Rinehart and Winston of Canada.
12. Mehrotra, Arvind Krishna. (2003). *The Illustrated History of Indian Literature in English*. C Hurst & Co Publishers Ltd.
13. Naik, M. K. (1982). *A History of Indian English Literature*. Sahitya Akademi.
14. Pisharoty, Sangeeta Barooah. (2020, Jul 19). Aruni Kashyap on Assam's Rich Literary
15. Tradition, Tejimola and Political Conflict. *The Wire*. Retrieved from http:// www.thewire.in
16. Rutland, Barry. (Ed.). (1997). *Gender and Narrative*. Carleton University Press.
17. Tauches, Kimberly. (2012). Transgendering: Challenging the "normal". In Steven
18. Seidman, Nancy Fischer and Chet Meeks (Eds.), *Introducing the New Sexuality Studies* (pp. 173-179). Routledge.
19. Vanita, Ruth. (2011). *Queering India: Same-Sex Love and Eroticism in Indian Culture and Society*. Routledge.

# Unearthing Queer Narratives in Assamese Writings of the Twentieth Century

**Stuti Goswami**

## Abstract

Fiction in the Assamese language has a rich history as well as a broad range of development. In the post-independent era, Assamese fiction has undergone several stages of evolution. Within this time frame of post-independent Assamese fiction (that spans roughly nine decades) one witnesses a certain degree of monotony in the depiction of sexuality. Usually, the characters and depictions are of heterosexuality with not much emphasis on rainbow communities. However, there are certain exceptions over the decades and this essay will focus on a few authors in whose short stories and novels there is an exploration of the dynamics of queer existence and relationships. The thrust of the essay would be a synchronic as well as diachronic reading of queer narratives in Assamese fiction in the post-independent era. It will also adopt a new historicist approach to explore the socio-political-cultural dynamics that influenced the writing as well as reception of queer narratives in Assamese fiction. The selection of time-frame (of post-independent) is owing to the major social-historical-cultural changes that came over Assamese society after the attainment of Indian independence.

**Keywords:** *Assamese, new historicism, synchronic and diachronic.*

## Introduction

Michel Foucault in *The History of Sexuality* (1976) discusses how sexuality-based categories of identity did not exist till well into the nineteenth century although sexuality and representations of sexuality far precede this era. However, in the Indian context, categorisations of sexuality and the taboos as well as the homophobia attached to the same could be said to originate in the British colonial rule in India. In the colonial period, non-heteronormative sexual categories were viewed as taboo, and this was both a carryover from British Victorian morality and a skewed idea of sexual promiscuity in non-European cultures that was imposed on British colonies. As Enze Han and Joseph O' Mahoney show in *British Colonialism and the Criminalization of Homosexuality: Queens, Crime and Empire* (2018) from the 1860s,

> the British Empire spread a specific set of legal codes and common law throughout its colonies including prominent examples of criminal codes of India and Queensland, both of which specifically criminalized mate-to-male sexual relations. (Enze and O'Mahoney, 2018, 3).

The Indian Penal Code of 1860, the first of its kind across all colonies of the British empire[1], initiated prosecution of homosexual acts or same-sex relationships, thereby othering queer normativity in British India.[2] [3] Even in the imposition or the application of the law, however, there was unevenness between the natives and the British.[4] This furthered the othering of homosexuality in natives as unnatural. Not only imposition of law but support (and acceptance) towards such measures of the government increased and thereby came to be embedded in the thoughts of the ruled native classes. A

---

1 Martin L. Friedland writes about this in "Codification in the Commonwealth: Earlier Efforts" in Commonwealth Law Bulletin 18, no. 3 (1992)

2 Anjali R. Arondekar examines colonial jurisprudence and sexuality in For the Record: On the Sexuality and the Colonial Archive in India, Duke University Press, 2009.

3 Suparna Bhaskaran examines the factors that contributed towards British government's anti-sodomy laws in India in 1860

4 In 1844, an Indian eunuch named Khairati was convicted of sodomy despite there being no evidence that proved her 'crime. The only evidence that was used against Khairati was that he dressed up as a woman often and displayed certain signs of a sodomite. (Ruhnke, 2016, 6) In contrast British soldiers were given much less punishment for what was termed their "immoral tendencies". (Arondekar, 2009, 85)

major factor that precipitated such notions is the resurrection and appropriation of certain Hindu texts by the British in an attempt to create a "civil legal tradition fit for their new realm from its own history". (Kemp, 2019, 18) The Sikh and Islamic communities had their respective religious laws unlike the Hindus and therefore there were serious attempts under the government's patronage to create a narrative (on same sex relationships and their unnaturalness or their impurity) that was sourced from the past of the natives itself. A major text used for this purpose was the ancient Hindu text *Manusmriti* that was upheld to highlight the notion that same sex relations reduced the purity of men. (Kemp, 2019, 18)[5] In addition to this, the emergence of anti-homosexuality notions (and an accompanying homophobia) in British India was also caused by an eagerness (a necessity?) among many among the native population to acquiesce to the ideology of the rulers for their social advancement and acceptance and the expansion of Christianity in British India. In his BBC News article "Why legalising gay sex in India is not a Western idea" (2018) Vikas Pandey cites Harbans Mukhia,

> The British brought their own rules to India, including Section 377... This law was enforced by them but it didn't conform with India's attitude toward homosexuality. It was more to do with their Christian belief systems. (Pandey, 2018, para 5)

As with England, in colonial India too "understandings of homosexuality were reframed through the rhetoric of the purity campaign". (Ruhnke, 2016, 4) Literatures produced in British India during the colonial period barely have explicit depiction of same-sex relationships or homoerotic desires. On the contrary one sees attempts that "represented" homosexuality and homoerotic desires "by means of absences, slips and gaps in the narration". (Rajesh and Venkatesan, 2015, 175) Thus in the colonial period, the

5 Kemp argues that the issue is here more of purity than of sin. After sex (between two men) the expectation is for the men to cleanse themselves in the river by dipping with all the clothes on

literature produced spoke majorly through silences on same sex relationships–whether affectional or sexual.[6] Ismat Chugtai's 1942 short story "Lihaaf" is a powerful instance of a text that speaks of same sex relations that are sexual in nature. The narrator's aunt Begum Jaan is spurned by the Nawaab, her much-older husband, who has an affection for younger healthy males (of slender waists). As a domino effect, the lonely Begum Jaan forges an intimate relationship with her maid and masseur Rabbu. But the narrator, then a young girl too, falls prey to Begum Jaan's near-insatiable sexual hunger urge that leaves her traumatised. The short story was controversial when it was first published in *Adab-i-Latif* . But all the scenes depicting erotic or sexual overtones are suggestive rather than explicit, but those are very powerful.

Another possible instance could be Rabindranath Tagore's novel *Gora* that focuses on the intimacy of male bonding between the characters of Gormohan and Binoy Bhushan. From the outset the two characters, presented as childhood friends and playmates, are shown to be constantly together–the two go to college together and return, study together on the terrace, eat together and often fall asleep on the mat together. Binoy even keeps a photograph of Gormohan on the wall of his hut to see his friend whenever he is not physically present. However, their intimacy is more of 'closeted homosexual desires' as Rajesh James and Satyaraj Venkatesan try to establish in their paper "Transgressing the Borders: Ambiguous Queer Spots, Homoerotic Silences and Tagore's Gora and Two Sisters". The writers say, Tagore "can only represent such relationships as a slippage between friendship and ambiguous but dynamic same-sex desires". (James and Venkatesan, 2015, 179)

These two instances show how the silences between the lines make the queer an object of study and promotion of queer as a political

6 Ruth Vanita and Saleem Kidwai have argued in Same -Sex Love in India: Readings from Literature and History (2021), in the Indian context particularly such concerns have existed from ancient times, as we witness their depiction in epic literature and mythology all through Bhakti movement in medieval India and Urdu literary universe in subsequent times.

subject. The act of depicting sexual same-sex relationship in each text is a political statement by both writers, a voice of assertion of the existence of such relationships and a voice of protest against the impositions on such relationships. However, it is equally true that a reading of literature produced in pre-independent India (and in Assam) through the lens of queer studies would attempt reconstructions of traditional gender roles, re-imagining supposedly heterosexual characters in literature as "closeted" gay/ lesbian lovers and agitating to make formerly marginal forms of pleasure and desire in to perfectly acceptable, mainstream ones. (Mohan, 2002, 124)

## Unearthing Queer Voices in British Assam in the Twentieth Century

In British Assam, as in other parts of British India of the twentieth century, "heterosexual ideology dominates the hegemonic knowledge production of spaces" as far as literature was concerned. (Hazarika, 2022, para. 4) A major development in Assamese language and literature at the turn of the century and the early twentieth century is the emergence of a print culture. However, even a cursory reading through of the earliest journals and magazines reveal considerable silence in even subtle indications towards same sex relationships that are sexual in nature although friendships between members of the same gender are referred to on multiple occasions. This writer examined all available issues of *Jonaki* (1901 and 1902)[7], *Chetona* (1920 and 1921) and *Awahon* (1929 and 1930)[8] Out of these, there is a short story "Tirutar Atmakatha" by Nakul Chandra Bhuyan published in the May 1920 issue of *Chetona.* The narrator of this piece is a married woman from a flourishing household who mentions two servants from among the servants of the household: a Kachari boy who is very dear to her husband and for whom the servant boy can give up his life and a young girl (who is of unknown origins, having been found by

---

7 This writer headed a short term students' research project of digitization of Jonaki (1889-1903) in 2022, the same can be accessed at www.assamarchive.org

8 Source: www.assamarchive.org

the narrator's father afloat on the flooded waters of the river) who stays with the narrator all the time. Further, the narrator says how once, they spied a youth from the town frequenting the area near their farm. But after a few days, when that youth was no longer to be seen, the narrator's husband's behaviour towards his wife seemed to change. He became sad and almost detached to the goings-on around him, as if burdened by thoughts he could not share with his wife. The narrator mentions that he ceased to kiss his wife like before and even stopped coming to her room.[9] Though nowhere is it explicitly stated, the hints of the young Kachari servant boy's close attachment to the narrator's husband and the servant girl's attachment to the narrator throws subtle hints at a same-sex bonding that is not filial and is more than affectional. At the end of the story, the husband's detachment from his wife is shown as his jealousy towards what he perceives to be an illicit relationship between his wife and the servant boy, thus pointing towards heterosexual desires. But the reference to the husband turning detached with the absence of the "sohoria deka" or the youth from the town is interesting. At several places in the story, indications of same-sex desires can be discerned though the story's ending has conventionally heterosexual pointers.

The concept of a close bosom friend of the same gender is presented in terms of *sakhi* and *sakha* (for female and male friendships respectively) in Bhakti literature of pre-British India.[10] In the writings of Jyotiprasad Agarwala, specially his plays, bonding and female bonding are widely seen though the emphasis is more on their affectional relationship

---

9 Bhuyan, Nakul Chandra. "Tirutar Atmakatha" ("Self Reflections of a Woman"). Chetana, Issue 9. Spring 1920, eds. Chandranath Sarma and Ambikacharan Raichoudhury, p. 412. Digitizing অসম. www.assamarchive.org

10 Across India, Bhakti literature abounds in male devotees singing paeans to male gods, and often in such praises in the form of songs and hymns the male devotees, the devotees are seen to pine for the male gods or male avatars of gods. Ruth Vanita and Saleem Kidwai explore this in Same-Sex Love in India (2000) while Rima Bhattacharyya explores this fluidity of devotion and desire in "The Transgendered Devotee: Ambiguity of Gender in Devotional Poetry", Indian Journal of Gender Studies, Vol. 25 Issue 2, 2018.

than sexual.[11] In Jyotiprasad Agarwala's play *Karengor Ligiri* (1937) we witness such a bond between Sundor Kunwor or Prince Sundor and his friend Anangaram. Though both are shown to engage in heterosexual relationships (Anangaram with Kanchan who in turn is married to Prince Sundor) the relationships never materialise. There is, however, in the play a song that Anangaram sings for (and to) Sundor, "Mure Jeevanare Sokha Krishno" that loosely translates to "O Krishna, the *sakha* of my life". The song is a paean to the physical beauty and the virtues of Lord Krishna with whom Prince Sundor is equated. This interpretation of course treads an ambiguous path, as nowhere is any explicit reference to any sexual tension and/or desire between Sundor and Anangaram. At the same time, Sundor is shown to be averse to marriage as he proclaims himself to be a man not interested in marriage (with a woman) and procreation but in the pursuit of knowledge. The song echoes the paeans to male gods of Bhakti literature, and it is in this aspect that Jyotiprasad Agarwala's play finds mention in this discussion.

Bishnu Prasad Rava in his short prose piece *"Haragouri Nritya ba Ardhanariswarar Nritya "* writes about the creation of *Ardhanariswar* in Hindu mythology.[12] Although this is a tale from mythology not specific to Assam or Assamese culture, the retelling in Assamese language shows the writer's attempts to localize a pan-Indian mythological tale for a native (Assamese) audience. Of course, this is not the first instance of retelling of mythological tales in Assamese language in the magazines of the early twentieth century and yet the choice of the tale–one that connotes gender that is gender fluid and non-binary—is interesting.

---

11 Instances of male and female same-sex bonding in Jyotiprasad's plays are to be found in Sonit Konwari , Karengor Ligiri, and Nimati Koina.

12 Rava, Bishnu Prasad. "Haragouri Nritya ba Ardhanariswarar Nritya". Bishnu Prasad Rava Rasana Sambhar,Vol. I., eds. Jogesh Das and Dr Sarbeswar Bora, Rabha Rasanawoli Prakashan Sangha, 1989,reprint 2019

## Selected Readings of Queer Voices in post-independent Assamese literature.

It is interesting that though post-independence Assamese language writings are still majorly shrouded in silence continue on queer voices, a few short stories down the decades do illuminate upon the queer universe in subtle or not-so-subtle ways. This, however, is particularly witnessed in the later decades of the twentieth century and the early part of the twenty first. In this context mention might be made of the short story "Suwali Hostelor Egoraki Lesbian" ("A Lesbian in a Girl's Hostel") by Gobinda Prasad Sarma that touches upon the perceptions on and towards lesbian relationships and a lesbian individual in a girl's hostel, Apurba Kumar Sarma's "Asamajik" ("Un-Social") that explores the connotations—personal and societal—attached to non-binary non- heteronormative relationships, Moushumi Kandali's "Tritiyatwar Galpa" ("The Tale of Thirdness") that explores the psychology of a homosexual man, pressured by society's rigid and conventional (patriarchal) parameters of sexuality and Bipul Khataniar's "Hijra" a story that explores the members of the community generically (and usually pejoratively) labelled as 'hijra'. All these and several other significant short stories feature in the collection of short stories *Tritiyo Akaash: Emuthi Nirbasito Sutigalpa—Prasanga LGBTQ ("The Third Firmament: Selected Short Stories on LGBTQ)* (2022)[13] compiled and edited by Dr Prapti Thakur with an introduction by Dr Pori Hiloidari. This significant book is the first of its kind in the Assamese language that touch upon or engage with queer matters in their narratives. In the introduction to this book, Hiloidari writes short stories by authors like Sneh Devi and Gobinda Prasad Sarma not only mark the initial phase of queer voices in post-independent Assam, but also indicate the fact that such matters could be and were being addressed in a conservative society like Assam. In this significant introduction Hiloidari has succinctly introduced briefly each of the thirty one stories included in this

[13] The names of the short stories and books in English in this chapter (mentioned in brackets) are loose translations only, made by this author.

collection besides locating these stories in the broader discourses of gender and sexuality vis-à-vis queer experiences and identities. At the same time, the introduction posits it's discussion on the aspect of social, particularly the class and caste dynamics, that influence not only queer relationships and identity but also the portrayal as well as reading of such relationships and identities through literature. This book is significant also for its attempt at identity assertion of the queer universe in what is often perceived to be 'mainstream' literary discursive practices. At the same time, each of these stories focus more on a sensitive portrayal and understanding of queer experience and identity—instead of focusing on sexual and physical aspects of queer relationships, something that Hiloidari too points out in her introduction.

This chapter eschews a detailed discussion on the thrity one short stories in this collection and instead offers a discussion on four short stories—all written and published in the twenty first century—in Assamese language These writers feature in the collection mentioned above though these short stories (except for one) are different from the one's included in this collection. The short stories taken up for further discussion in the next section are—Jayanta Saikia's "Sagaraor Gondh", Arup Kumar Nath's "Baazikor" first published in the magazine *Satsari* (2007), Sanjib Pol Deka's "Nukuwa Kahini" from his collection of stories *Barmajhili* (2020) later reprinted in T*ritiyo Akash* (2022)[14]

## A Brief Discussion on Selected Short Stories in Assamese

As the decades pass by, queer voices become visible in the literary spectrum in the Assamese language. In post-independent Assam, we witness the emergence of a few writers who speak on LGBTQ+ issues in a relatively direct manner. This chapter eschews individual discussion on several short stories of post-independence Assamese literature this chapter would look with keener lens the following

[14] This short story is included in the collection Tritiyo Akash

short stories— "Nukuwa Kahini" by Sanjib Pol Deka, "Sagaror Gondh" by Jayanta Saikia and "Baazikor" by Arup Kumar Nath.

Sanjib Pol Deka's short story "Nukuwa Kahini" ("The Untold") is the story of a young boy from an impoverished family who is trapped into sexual exploitation at the hands of a slightly older gay man in his village. This older man stays apart from his family as he helps him monetarily and gifts him clothes etc., takes him to visit different places, and introduces him as his 'younger brother' to people. The only demand (unstated but powerfully implied) he makes on the young boy is for him to sleep with him at night. This continues for several years—from the time the young boy is on the verge of teenage to almost-stepping out of his teenage years. When he is younger (barely a teen) he does not realise what happens at night when he is asleep, but soon enough he begins to realise what happens but he is embarrassed and ignorant enough to pretend to remain asleep—this continues for several years. It is much later that this young boy one day chances upon a newspaper report and realises that what he has been going through for the past time is a wrongful act. The young boy is never comfortable with this arrangement, but he feels entrapped in this arrangement, as he tries to (desires to) but is not able to find a means to escape. Meanwhile, the man's family not only look down on him, they insult him in the worst possible means , not sparing his family either. But the sexual exploitation continues and all through the story it is made evident how the young boy, who eventually turns out to be narrator of the story, a successful journalist recounting in an inebriated state his bitter past experiences, never enjoys these sexual encounters. The young boy is shown as a victim and the victimizer, is also hinted at as one kind of victim of sexual frustration because his sexuality is constantly suppressed by a heteronormative society. Much later, it is revealed (recounted) that that man is married (to a woman) and unlike the younger man he was when he would look down on the humbler folk of the village, now has been humbled and is living a pitiable existence.

This short story cannot be written off entirely or solely as a story of sodomy but it is of sexual exploitation between members of the same gender, of sexual suppression in a heteronormative society, of the widespread homosexuality that—realised or unrealised—exists in the rural areas. Although the story is set in Assam, the same can be applied to any part of rural India. The title of the story emphasises on that which is not stated, on the silences between the lines as homosexual relationships—whether consensual or exploitative are seen both as an aberration or an abnormality and also as something not to be spoken about. The descriptions of sexual encounters(exploitation) are evocative enough though there is no explicit description.

Arup Kumar Nath's short story "Baazikor" ("The Snake Charmer") is a story that centers around sexual exploitation between an older man and younger boy—again the setting is a village in Assam. On the pretext of taking the narrator Amar Chaliha to see the snake charmer (in the nearby town—the narrator had never seen a town before that) the victimiser Jitu Dutta or Jitu da takes the narrator to a deserted tree house in a deserted field, and provides the narrator his first experience of sex and sexual experience. Unlike the previous short story, however, in this story the narrator becomes an active (probably equal probably the more desirous one in certain moments) participant in the homosexual relationship. This short story too is written/narrated in flashback (in retrospect) with the narrator now an established bureaucrat and that da a powerless man—and yet the narrator feels unmistakably the power of//and allure of those eyes. The English equivalent of the word "baazikor" is magician. However, as the metaphor of the snake and snake charmer is consistently used—the male sexual organ (the penis) is referred to as snake as well—this writer has termed the English title of the short story as "The Snake Charmer". The story shows how the childhood experience of sex leaves the narrator both scarred and awakened to the pleasures of sexual experience. Years later when left behind all alone, the desertion leaves him devastated and with a suppressed thirst for sexual and sensual pleasure from a same-sex relationship. In the present of the story the narrator engages in a heterosexual marriage and is shown to be fully in love and devoted to his wife with a 'happy' family with a wife and children and successful life. Here the narrator's sexuality is suppressed sexuality and he bowing to social pressure (and as it is implied in loneliness at the desertion of his male partner) by marrying a woman and fathering children indicates his bisexual rather than homosexual tendencies. This story, unlike the previous one, adopts an ambivalent stance towards his male partner who is portrayed more as a 'magician' or 'snake charmer'. In this story the snake is also a symbol of the phallus. Both short stories depict phallocentric suppression.

In Sanjib Pol Deka's short story, the victim victimizer relation is evident—the narrator is an unwilling participant in the prolonged homosexual relationship which has overtones of sexual exploitation. In Arup Kumar Nath's short story, the narrator too has a prolonged sexual relationship with his senior but unlike the previous story here the narrator both dreads and somewhere desires (despite his claims to the contrary) the physical presence and proximity of Jitu da. The phallocentric suppression is also a cause of trauma (childhood trauma that remains unhealed in later life too) for the protagonists of both the stories.[15] Both narrators express/reveal their helplessness and inability to come out of their quagmire—for the narrator in Sanjib Pol's story it is economic constraint while in Arup Kumar Nath's story there is no evident cause barring the psychological (and sexual) grip //psychosexual grip the narrator feels himself in the relationship.

Jayanta Saikia's story "Sagarar Gondh" ("The Smell of the Sea") on the other hand focuses on a lesbian relationship. Here the narrator is a student of Banaras Hindu University when he meets two German ladies Martha and Margaret in a relationship—over time, through email communications (the story is set in the late nineties of the last century as smartphones do not mark their presence as yet). Over the course of a few years the narrator and one of these two women are in constant touch over emails and then letters and postcards and pictures. During this time period the two women go through tumultuous relationship, then break up, then the correspondent

15 In many ways in both the stories the two narrators experience post-traumatic stress disorder.

Martha marries a co-worker (a man, once again engaging in a heterosexual relationship), has a child, then is divorced and at the end, the narrator learns that the two Marth and Margaret are together again co-parenting their child. The narrator too returns home (Assam) and marries his partner (presumably a woman)—the narrator all through seems to be addressing this lover—thus the narrative of the story is that of a text within a text—where the narrator addresses (and relays—to his lover) his experiences with Marth and Margaret as Martha relays and narrates *her* experiences (relationship and love) to the narrator. In this story too, the character engages into a heterosexual marriage though that relationship does not last for long and she reverts to her relation (lesbian) with her lover Margaret. At the end of the story the narrator returns home (Assam) and marries his lover (a woman). However, there is a tone of melancholy in the narrator's voice all through—there is enough hint of a tension or strain or at least distance in his relationship with his lover (with whom he is in a long-distance relationship with and who is in his home state). The exact reason for this detachment (at some level) and distance is not clearly stated in the story—that is left unsaid/unstated. That is left for the reader to interpret.

These three short stories are written in the first person, giving a personal touch as well as pathos in the narrative in equal measures. The homosexual relationship is a fact in each of the stories—while in one the narrator (the protagonist) is an observer who literally narrates a lesbian relationship based in another country the other two stories are set in Assam (rural Assam) and is a lived experience of the respective narrators. The stories also highlight how traumatic experiences of the past leave their imprint behind on the adult memory. They also highlight the wide-ranging ignorance regarding sexual suppression prevalent in rural areas that are often left unsaid or swept under the carpet and how patriarchy homogenizes sexual experience and identity into the rigid binary of male/female.

## Conclusion

A cursory reading of the history of writings in the Assamese language shows how queer voices have been increasingly heardandapparentas the years have passed by. This has been possible because of increasing visibility of as well as discussions on the queer universe in society—even a relatively traditional society as Assamese society—within the broader context of Indian society. One aspect that this chapter did not touch upon (and that this writer would like to explore further) is the queer tendencies in the folk literature of Assam. The myriad fabric of ethnicity in Assam and northeast India as a whole offers multiple possibilities of interpretation of queer experiences as well as queer expressions in the domain of folk narratives. At the same time this brief discussion on queer voices can be viewed in the broader perspective of queer narratives in India (n literature). The reading shows similar tendencies as pan-Indian grand narrative of queer identity and discursive practices and yet shows distinctiveness in the light of the distinct socio-cultural-economic-political dynamics of Assam as a region in the northeastern part of India.

## References:


1. Han, Enze Han and O' Mahoney, Joseph. (2018). *British Colonialism and the Criminalization of Homosexuality: Queens, Crime and Empire* (p. 3). Routledge.
2. Hazarika, Nizara. (2022). Transgressive Spatialities: Mapping Identity and Liminality in Contemporary Queer Narratives from Assam. *Rupkatha Journal. Volume 4 Issue 2,* 3.
3. James, R. and Venkatesan, S. (2015). Transgressing the Borders: Ambiguous Queer Spots, Homoerotic Silences and Tagore's *Gora* and *Two Sisters. The Appollonian. Vol. 2Issue 2,* 175.
4. Kemp, S. (2019). *How did British Colonialism influence the perception and representation of same-sex intimacies in Indian* (Master's thesis, Leiden Universiteit).
5. Mohan, Anupama. (2002). Queer Theory. *Critical Theory: Textual Application.* Ed: Sharmistha Panja (p.124) New Delhi: Worldview Publications.
6. Pandey, Vikas. (2018). Why legalising gay sex in India is not a Western idea. *bbc.com.*accessed 12 December 2022.
7. Ruhnke, Lauren. (2018). Constructing Native Homosexuality in British India. *Maneto: The Temple University Multi-Disciplinary Undergraduate Research Journal. 1.1,* 89.

# List of Contributors

(In Alphabetical Order)

**Anupom Kumar Hazarika**, born and raised in Golaghat, is an Assistant Professor of English at Cotton University, Assam. He received a BA in English and Mathematics from Debraj Roy College, Golaghat. He obtained an MA in English from Dibrugarh University and an MPhil in English from Gauhati University. Also, he earned a Master's degree in Mass Communication from Tezpur University. At present, Hazarika is pursuing a part-time PhD at IIT Guwahati. His research interests are Indian English Literature, queer literature and science fiction. Hazarika has had poetry published in CC&D Magazine, Nagaland Page, Spark, Terror House Magazine, The Assam Tribune, and The Chakkar. His essays on bullying, gender, Harry Potter movies, mobile applications, poetry, science fiction have appeared in various publications, including In Plainspeak, Live Mint, Pink Advocate, The Assam Tribune, The Chakkar, and The Eastern Today.

**Anjuman Ara Begum, PhD** is Associate Professor at Royal School of Law and Administration, the Assam Royal Global University, Guwahati, Assam. She has over 17 years of multi-disciplinary experience of working as researcher, academic, journalist, trainer, campaigner and consultant working on the broad themes of law, gender, peace and conflict, human rights, right to information, freedom of expression, digital rights and cyber security. She worked with several national and international NGOs, universities and closely associated with women rights groups in India and abroad.

**Alimuddin Ahmed** holds a MSW degree and presently works as a professional Makeup Artist.

**Deepshikha Carpenter**, Ph.D, is Head (i/c), Department of Social Work, Mahapurusha Srimanta Sankaradeva Viswavidyalaya, Guwahati, Assam. She specialises in Social Work and Gender Studies. Her interests of research work are Social Work Education,

Gender, Crime and Violence and Disability Studies. She has published a number of articles in books and journals.

**Namami Sharma**, PhD is currently working as a faculty member in the Department of Social Work, Tezpur University. Her areas of interests are ecology, traditional knowledge systems, community organisation and Gender issues. In recent times, she has been exploring the arena of Nutrition with specific focus on equity specific nutrition. Namami has several years of experience of working in the rural areas of Uttarakhand, Madhya Pradesh and Chattisgarh. During her engagements in these locations, she was primarily working with communities and peoples institutions with specific focus on their natural resources. Emerging out of her field experiences, she located her MPhil research among the Baiga community in Madhya Pradesh and positioned her Phd Research with the Monpa community in Arunachal Pradesh. The underlying aim of her engagements has been an inclusive society. As she was manouvering across various forums, she found that the term inclusivity excludes certain groups and one group that continues to be obliterated is the non-binary gender identities. That's when, she began looking at the gaps in the understanding and stereotypes concerning these identities. This article is a step towards that effort.

**Nilakshi Goswami**, PhD is a Fulbright Nehru-Postdoctoral Research Fellow 2020-2021 at the Department of Anthropology, Boston University. She has been a recipient of several prestigious awards, viz., the California Archival State Award 2022, The German Historical Institute Washington, the Summer Institute Fellowship on Genocide Studies and Prevention at the Cohen Center for Holocaust and Genocide Studies, Keene State College, the CURA (Institute of Culture, Religion, and World Affairs) Fellowship 2021-2022, Boston University, Sahapedia-UNESCO Fellowship 2018, and Graduate Student Caucus Award 2016, NeMLA (Northeast Modern Languages Association). She is currently working at Girijananda Chowdhury University as an Assistant Professor in the Department of English. Nilakshi holds a PhD in English Literature from The English and Foreign Languages University and a BA and MA (English Literature) from Delhi University. Her work focuses on Southeast Asian Studies, Gender and Sexuality Studies, popular culture and performance arts, and efficacies, affects and values associated with image, performance, and gender identity.

**Neitsope U Thopi** has been working with northeast Network since 2005. She is a keyboard player with the local church choir and has been part of Chizami Youth Society for a long time in Nagaland. Currently she spearheads the Chizami Weaves unit of Nenterprise a community-based weavers collective in Nagaland.

**Panna Paul** is currently working as a lecturer of English in Gurukul Senior Secondary School. His areas of studies include Queer Studies and Queer Literature from the Indian Sub-Continent. He is also the Co-Editor of Yawp ! the only English Little Magazine dedicated to the propagation and promotion of English Literature in the Barak Valley of Assam, India. He has completed his M.Phil and is currently preparing for his PhD.

**Samhita Barooah**, PhD, has been working in the field of Social Work Practice, Research and Education for almost 2 decades in Assam, Meghalaya, Nagaland and Rural Madhya Pradesh. Sammy has worked in media as a freelance journalist and academia as a faculty for more than a decade in North East India. She started Haiku Home, a homestay in Guwahati in 2011 to support zer retired parents and an initiative called QueerUp2020 during the lockdown period to co-create support, solidarity and sustainability with the vibrant queer community of Assam. Sammy's film on zer queer identity titled 'Being Sammy' is made by Rainbow Stories, The Story Circle, Theatre Alliance and US Consulate Kolkata. Currently Sammy teaches at the Department of Social Work, Tezpur University as an Assistant Professor and lives in Tezpur.

**Silba Marak** is pursuing her PhD from the Department of English at North Eastern Hill University (NEHU) Tura Campus, Meghalaya.

**Somava Das** is a PhD Scholar in the Department of Journalism and Mass Communication, Assam University Silchar. Her areas of work are Memory Studies, Queer Popular Culture, Media studies, Film studies and Queer Studies.

**Stuti Goswami**, PhD is an Assistant Professor of English at The Assam Royal Global University, Guwahati, India. Her areas of specialisation are Translation Studies, British Assam, Literary Studies, Climate Writing and Traditional Knowledge Systems, and Literature of North East India. She has delivered talks and chaired academic sessions at several national and international (physical and online) conferences. She has about forty academic publications to her credit and as a creative writer and translator, has nearly a hundred publications in Assamese and English (both in original and in translation). She has/shares editing credits in the following works: Essentially Speaking: Biographical Snapshots (Gauhati University Press, 2015), Warp and Weft: Makers of Modern Assam (National Book Trust, India, 2018), Pollen Grain (Red River Press, New Delhi, 2022), Beseiged (Assam Institute of Translation, an imprint of Asam Sahitya Sabha, 2022). In 2022 she led a digitization project of the Assamese language magazine Jonaki (1889-1903). This project and the funding institution The Assam Royal Global University features as a partner institution in the community digitization project Digitizing অসম.

# Appendix: 1: Advisory for ensuring the welfare of Transgender Persons

राष्ट्रीय मानव अधिकार आयोग
मानव अधिकार भवन, सी–ब्लॉक,
जीपीओ कम्पलेक्स आईएनए, नई दिल्ली–110 023 भारत
National Human Rights Commission
Manav Adhikar Bhawan, C-Block,
GPO Complex, INA, New Delhi-110023 India

No. R-51/ 2/ 2023 - PRPP (RU-2), dated 15th September, 2023

**Advisory for ensuring the welfare of Transgender Persons**

Under the Protection of Human Rights Act, 1993, the National Human Rights Commission (NHRC) is entrusted with the responsibility of protecting and promoting human rights of all human beings in the country. In this regard, one of the primary concerns of the Commission is about discrimination faced by transgender persons in the country.

2. The rights of the Transgender persons have gained recognition and legal validity through various judgments of the Supreme Court. A landmark development was the enactment of the Transgender Persons (Protection of Rights) Act, 2019, which explicitly aimed to safeguard and uphold the rights of transgender individuals. Despite these legal advancements, transgender persons continue to grapple with discrimination in multiple facets of life. This discrimination manifests in various forms such as employment disparities, limited access to healthcare, and exclusion from social circles.

3. To address these challenges, the Commission has approved an 'Advisory for ensuring the welfare of Transgender Persons' to the Union and State governments, containing a set of recommendations, designed to enhance the welfare and rights of transgender persons.

4. All concerned authorities of the Union/ State Government(s)/ UT Administration(s) are advised to implement the recommendations made in the advisory in letter and spirit, and to send an Action Taken Report (ATR) within two months to keep the Commission informed of the progress in implementing the advisory.

[ Bharat Lal ]
Secretary General

**Enclosed:** Advisory for ensuring the welfare of transgender persons

1. Secretary
   Deptt. of Social Justice & Empowerment
   C-Wing, Shastri Bhawan, New Delhi - 110 001

2. Secretary
   Ministry of Corporate Affairs, A" Wing, Shastri Bhawan,
   New Delhi - 110 001.

3. All Chief Secretaries/ Administrators (all States & UTs)

फोन : 91-11-24663211, 24663212 फैक्स : 91-11-24663262
Phone : 91-011-24663211, 24663212, Fax : 91-011-24663262, E-mail : sgnhrc@nic.in, Website : www.nhrc.nic.in

## Advisory for Ensuring the welfare of Transgender Persons

### Education

i. Necessary steps may be taken to ensure access to education to transgender persons. Authorities may consider formulating a policy to address the issues of violence, discrimination and their harassment at educational institutions. The Education Department of all States/ UTs as an interim measure to advise educational institutes in their respective jurisdictions to protect gender-nonconforming students from bullying, harassment or other forms of violence.

ii. The State Governments/ UTs to ensure that in every district, an anti-discrimination cell is set up at the district level for transgenders, and also, to ensure the setting up of a monitoring committee/ cell at educational institutions to address the issues of prejudices, discrimination, sexual abuse and other violence against transgender persons.

iii. The State Governments to take necessary steps to make all educational institutions "inclusive" for transgender students.

iv. Transgender students are not to be discriminated against in higher studies, and suitable provision for providing financial assistance to Transgender students pursuing Degree/ Diploma/ PG courses may be ensured.

v. Provision for scholarship and free education be formulated for transgender students.

### Healthcare:

i. Set up medical boards at the district level to assist transgenders.

ii. In every district civil hospital, necessary provisions to be made for consultation, treatment, counseling for sex reassignment surgery, and, the following steps may also be considered;

   a. A suitable amount may be provided to the members of the transgender community who want to opt for a sex change operation; or,

b. Free sex reassignment surgery in government hospitals may be provided.

**Employment:**

i. "Third Gender" as an identity category may be added for people of transgender community seeking civil service jobs to enable them to apply and appear in entrance examinations.

ii. All the agencies involved in document verification may be advised to verify and accept the document even if the name or photo of the transgender person vary with the original documents on time bound manner, provided the candidate has obtained the Transgender Certificate.

iii. Adequate steps may be taken to protect transgender persons from any form of violence or harassment at workplaces, and anti-discrimination policies be implemented at all levels.

iv. Sensitization programmes for other employees on sexual orientation and gender identity may be organized regularly.

v. A Grievance Redressal Cell be set up in the organization wherever they are employed to deal with the issues of transgender employees, in which at least one transgender person may be included, wherever possible.

vi. State to prioritize skill development training and better occupational opportunities to transgender persons.

vii. Wide publicity to the National Career Service Portal be given amongst transgender community.

viii. Loan at interest subvention basis may be extended to transgender persons to help them set up their own businesses.

ix. District administration to extend help to enable transgender persons to form Self Help Groups through which they can get bank loans to start livelihood activities.

**Promoting Inclusivity:**

i. All forms for whatever purpose, which require candidates to indicate their sex, must provide 'third gender' as a category in the options.

ii. All public places should have separate washrooms for transgenders.

iii. Provide an exclusive platform for transgender persons to showcase their talent in cultural events.

iv. Old age home facilities be considered for the transgender community.

**Welfare**

i. Single trans child of a deceased government employee or pensioner, may be treated as an unmarried daughter for the family pension and other benefits.

ii. Transgender persons should be allowed to inherit ancestral agricultural land.

iii. Transgender welfare board may be established as mandated under the Section 10 (1) of the Transgender Persons (Protection of Rights) Rules, 2020, framed for implementing the Transgender Persons (Protection of Rights) Act, 2019.

iv. The concerned Ministry should ensure the timely release of the funds allocated to Garima Greh. In addition, the queries considering the disbursement of funds may be dealt with by proper mechanisms and handholding support be given to complete the requisite formalities to resolve such grievances.

v. The Insurance Companies may be advised to consider and accept the Transgender Certificate issued by the appropriate authority for document verification purposes.

vi. The Ministry of Corporate Affairs may consider incorporating welfare activities of transgender persons explicitly in the Schedule VII of the Companies Act, 2013, which provides the list of activities that can be included for making expenditures for Corporate Social Responsibilities activities.

vii. Adequate steps may be taken to deal with the complaints of sexual harassment of transgender persons.

viii. Multi-purpose identity cards may be provided to the transgenders to help them access government schemes and other benefits.

ix. Reach out to the family member of Transgenders through Anganwadi workers to sensitize them about trans-children.

x. Public to be sensitized through educational campaigns.

**Grievance Redressal**

i. Set up a Transgender Protection Cell under the Director General of Police or his/her nominee in the State to monitor cases of offences against Transgender Persons in accordance with the provision of the Transgender Persons (Protection of Rights) Act, 2019 and the Transgender Persons (Protection of Rights) Rules, 2020.

ii. One officer in every police station be designated as focal point for Transgenders.

******